Words of Hope

A DECADE OF ENDURING SERMONS

DOUGLAS G. PRATT

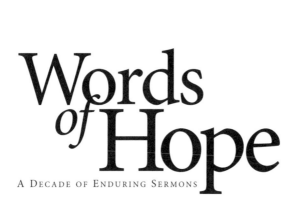

Words of Hope

A DECADE OF ENDURING SERMONS

A celebration of the preaching ministry of Pastor Doug Pratt

Unless otherwise identified, all scripture quotations in the publication are taken from the Holy Bible: New International Version® (NIV)®.

Foreword

Preach the word;
be prepared in season and out of season;
correct, rebuke and encourage—
with great patience and careful instruction.
– 2 TIMOTHY 4:2

The Senior Pastor of a large church wears many hats—chief executive officer, visionary, coach, mentor, teacher, fundraiser, servant—but his most public role, and greatest responsibility, is as a preacher of the Word of God.

So in celebrating a decade under the multifaceted leadership of Pastor Doug Pratt, it is no surprise that a book of his sermons was proposed as a memento of the occasion. But then the challenge began. How many messages? Which ones? We decided on ten—one for each year of his ministry at First Church—and a small committee then assembled the collection you have in your hand.

Ten messages, selected by committee: We are, after all, Presbyterians.

It is our prayer that God will use these words, which have spoken so powerfully to the congregation of this church over the last ten years, to bring hope, encouragement and instruction to many more in the years to come.

Table of Contents

A Scale Model of the Master

OCTOBER 3, 2004

The call to discipleship is so foundational to Pastor Pratt's ministry it is no surprise he wished to share this message with the congregation in his first year. This sermon is also included in his book, A Replica of Greatness.

Then God said, "Let us make humankind in our image, according to our likeness; and let them have dominion over the fish of the sea, and over the birds of the air, and over the cattle, and over all the wild animals of the earth, and over every creeping thing that creeps upon the earth."

27So God created humankind in his image, in the image of God he created them; male and female he created them. – GENESIS 1:26-27 (NRSV)

For I have set you an example, that you also should do as I have done to you. 16Very truly, I tell you, servants are not greater than their master, nor are messengers greater than the one who sent them. 17If you know these things, you are blessed if you do them. – JOHN 13:15-17 (NRSV)

Docked at the Charlestown Navy Yard in Boston, Massachusetts, is the sailing frigate *U.S.S. Constitution*. It is the oldest continually commissioned warship in the world. The *Constitution* was given the nickname "Old Ironsides" for its great strength, and its victories in numerous sea battles against French and North African pirate ships and against British warships in the War of 1812. Commissioned by Congress in 1794 and launched from a shipyard in Boston in 1797, the *Constitution* is one of the greatest examples from the era of the tall sailing ships. It was never defeated in battle. With its 44 cannons spewing flames and its three tall masts scraping the clouds, it was—and still is—an awesome sight. Hundreds of thousands of visitors each year climb its gangplanks, walk its decks, and stare upwards into its intricate rigging.

In the museum next to the permanent berth for "Old Ironsides," tourists can inspect a remarkable scale model of the great ship. The model is 8 feet long and 8 feet high, with intricate detail and craftsmanship. It was constructed by three talented model builders in Wellesley, Massachusetts. They put in over 62,000 hours of work to patiently recreate a faithful and accurate replica of the great ship. When the scale model was completed in 1932, it was purchased by the U.S. Navy to be housed in the new museum at the naval yard. To this day, model ship builders from around the world consider this replica to be one of the finest reproductions ever done. The Society of Model Shipbuilding holds its periodic meetings at the museum, so that hobbyists can see the model up close. Although the replica is less than 4% of the size of the original, it is a faithful and accurate reflection of the greatness that is the *U.S.S. Constitution*.

I believe that every Christian man and woman is invited by God to participate in a project very similar to that of those three craftsmen in 1932. We are called to make our lives into scale model replicas of the greatest

Person who has ever lived—Jesus of Nazareth. The task of building a smaller version of the Original is not one that can be accomplished in just 62,000 hours (a little more than seven years). It takes a lifetime. And the result, if undertaken with skill and diligence, is that you and I will become, at best, mere reflections of the indescribable greatness and glory of Jesus.

Why should this particular Man, a Galilean carpenter and itinerant preacher from twenty centuries ago, be chosen as the masterpiece which the entire race of mankind attempts to copy? Because His impact and His legacy are undeniable. In His own lifetime, His character was unimpeachable. Even His avowed enemies failed to find a single flaw to attack in Him. And since His death and resurrection, His influence has spread across the face of the earth like a tsunami. Witnesses historic and contemporary repeatedly confirm His place as the greatest, most influential Man who ever lived. Napoleon, the erstwhile conqueror of Europe, said this on his deathbed on St. Helena:

> I die before my time, and my body shall be given back to the earth and devoured by worms. What an abysmal gulf between my deep miseries and the eternal kingdom of Christ. I marvel that whereas the ambitious dreams of myself and of Alexander and of Caesar should have vanished into thin air, a Judean peasant, Jesus, should be able to stretch His hands across the centuries, and control the destinies of men and nations.

A contemporary—and decidedly non-Christian—source, *Newsweek* magazine, in its March 29, 1999 issue, introduced its cover story "2000 Years of Jesus" with this analysis: "Even by secular standards, Jesus is the dominant figure of Western culture."

Towering above all others across the centuries, surpassing the greatness of all those in every Hall of Fame, stands the greatest Man of all, Jesus Christ. He alone is worthy of our emulation, a fitting pattern for successful living.

It was God's intention from the very beginning of time that we humans, the pinnacle of His creation on planet Earth, would be scale models of Him. Genesis 1 records that original design in these simple words: "So God created humans in His image." The likeness or "image" He desires to see reflected in us on a smaller scale is not a physical one—for God has no body, and so it would be impossible to look like Him in any outward or material sense. Instead, the likeness was intended to be one of character and actions. We were meant to love one another as God loves us, to treat the creation He has placed us over with the same care that He has lavished upon His universe, and so on. But our sinful and selfish behavior has repeatedly marred and disfigured that image of God.

To reclaim His great replica, God came to us in the person of His Son, Jesus. His mission to Earth was to be our Savior, and also to be our great model or prototype: to show us what a perfect human life is to be like. In the 33 years Jesus walked the dust of the Middle East, He demonstrated without flaw the perfect "image of God" wrapped in flesh.

How can you and I begin to make ourselves into scale model replicas of this perfect Man? We undertake this project following the same process that the model ship builders in Massachusetts used. It requires first that we study the original in detail. The model builders spent hours poring over blueprints and plans for "Old Ironsides," and exploring the ship in person, inch-by-inch.

We must also—if we are serious about becoming replicas of greatness—study carefully the record of the life Jesus lived among us. We need to examine His four biographies in the New Testament (called Matthew, Mark, Luke and John), and also the writings of His contemporaries who knew Him personally (the letters of Peter, James, John, and other apostles).

The purpose of examining the life of Christ is not just historic interest or curiosity. We need to know how He lived, so that we can discern what He would do today, if He were in our place and time.

4

The "What Would Jesus Do?" question, which has recently become popularized and even trivialized by necklaces and wristbands and t-shirts and a thousand other reproductions, is actually a very profound question. It can't always be answered simply or easily, and not at all until we first look carefully at His life. The Lord Himself, the night before His death on a cross, told His disciples very clearly that He intended them to learn from His example and imitate Him: "I've given you an example that you should follow" (John 13:15).

The second step for model ship builders, after examining the original ship in detail, is to construct the replica piece-by-piece, inch-by-inch. With great patience and loving detail the model builders of the *Constitution* stitched the sails, cut and glued the deck boards, tied the rigging, and painted the portholes. Mistakes were commonly made, and the builders would have to remove the flawed piece or damaged sail and make it again until it was right. Such a quality scale model cannot be done quickly or hastily.

A consistent, faithful Christian life that truly reflects the character and the behavior of Jesus is likewise built piece-by-piece, day-by-day, through a painstaking lifetime of endeavor. When we mess up the model, when we make yet another mistake—as we all do—we just start over again and keep working to repair our errors, receiving His forgiveness and strength to keep on going.

What makes the scale model of the *U.S.S. Constitution* in Boston such a masterpiece of reproduction is that it is accurate not only in the outer visible details, but also in the hidden places. The craftsmen cared enough about getting it right that the inner parts of the ship which can't be seen by the casual tourist—the lower gun decks, the crew hammocks, the captain's cabin, even the structural supports for the hull—are all exact reproductions of the great ship.

That's what God wants us to do as well: to be living replicas of His

Son not only in the visible parts, but in the invisible as well. It's not enough to put on our Sunday smiles and pretend to be His followers in church. The Lord wants our hidden parts to be surrendered to Him as well. He cares just as much about our thought life and emotions, the way we are at home behind closed doors, the way we pray, what we read, how we talk, and how we get along with other people at work, as He cares about the way we look in church. And, of course, we can't fool Him like we can other people. He knows what's genuine and what's fake.

A true and enduring Christian outer life will only last if it's supported and sustained by a transformed inner life. Though invisible, it is that inner structure of prayer and thought and faith that supports us through the difficulties of life, just as the *U.S.S. Constitution* was able to hold up in battle and stormy seas only because of the strong inner structure of its hull.

The challenge to become a scale model of greatness is not one that many of us feel capable of achieving. It's a daunting task. And if God Himself had not beckoned each of us to try it, very few would ever consider such a goal. Some might object that it's far more than they desire. I don't aspire to greatness. I don't have any reason to want to become holy like Jesus. All I really want in life is just to be happy. Happiness, lasting joy, is what so many millions of people are chasing after in our world.

The ironic truth of life is that real, permanent happiness is never found by searching for it. Instead it's found by becoming what God has created us to be. The kind of joy that lasts, that no troubles or sorrows can take away, is the joy that is perfectly demonstrated in Jesus Himself. He alone has revealed to mankind the secret of true happiness.

If you want to be permanently, even eternally, happy, then bend your mind and will and effort to becoming a replica of Jesus Christ. The more you are like Him, in inner heart and outer actions, the more His unquenchable joy will bubble up in your heart.

Fighting for Liberty

JULY 3, 2005

*Pastor Pratt's grasp of ancient and modern history
often comes through in his choice of sermon illustrations—
and particularly so when we celebrate national holidays.*

*After the death of Moses the servant of the LORD, the LORD said to Joshua son
of Nun, Moses' aide: ²"Moses my servant is dead. Now then, you and all these
people, get ready to cross the Jordan River into the land I am about to give to
them—to the Israelites. ³I will give you every place where you set your foot,
as I promised Moses. ⁴Your territory will extend from the desert to Lebanon,
and from the great river, the Euphrates—all the Hittite country—to the Great
Sea on the west. ⁵No one will be able to stand up against you all the days of
your life. As I was with Moses, so I will be with you; I will never leave you
nor forsake you.*

⁶"Be strong and courageous, because you will lead these people to inherit the land I swore to their forefathers to give them. ⁷Be strong and very courageous. Be careful to obey all the law my servant Moses gave you; do not turn from it to the right or to the left, that you may be successful wherever you go. ⁸Do not let this Book of the Law depart from your mouth; meditate on it day and night, so that you may be careful to do everything written in it. Then you will be prosperous and successful. ⁹Have I not commanded you? Be strong and courageous. Do not be terrified; do not be discouraged, for the LORD your God will be with you wherever you go." – JOSHUA 1:1-9

He was a man who had been given an impossible job—and he knew how unworthy and inadequate he was. He had received little formal training to serve as a military commander, and his only experience in fighting had been years earlier, with mixed success. The people he had been given the commission to lead were not exactly an imposing force. Until recently they had been just submissive subjects groaning under the boot of an all-powerful ruler. Recently they had declared their freedom, but they knew that they would have to fight to maintain it. The actual troops serving under the general's command tended to be undisciplined, had received no formal training in the prevailing military tactics of their day, and were armed with hand-me-down weapons that were anything but state-of-the-art. The enemy army they faced was a crack force of professional soldiers. The stakes in the impending conflict could not have been higher: the survival of the young nation and its future security hung in the balance. In fact, the course of human history—and the success or failure of the ideals embodied in this new-born nation—depended on how well this inexperienced leader could guide his troops to victory.

That description fits the circumstances behind our scripture text for today: as the man Joshua was appointed by God Himself to be Supreme Commander of the army of the nation of Israel, newly-independent from the grip of the Pharaoh in Egypt and about to fight their first war to gain the Promised Land. There is every indication in our text that Joshua felt himself unprepared for the task, and intimidated and terrified by the odds against him. That alone explains why God speaks to Him over and over words of encouragement: "I will be with you … be strong and courageous … you will succeed … don't be terrified or discouraged … I will be with you."

The description I just gave you also applies equally to another man, nearly 3,000 years later, by the name of George Washington. He had been given the command of the fledgling Continental Army by the newly-formed Congress. The odds against him were just as imposing as those Joshua faced. And he knew how inadequate he was.

In accepting his commission on June 16, 1775, Washington stood before the Congress and said:

> I feel great distress from a consciousness that my abilities and military experience may not be equal to the extensive and important trust. As the Congress desires it, I will enter upon the momentous duty, and exert every power I possess in their service and for the support of the glorious Cause… But I this day declare with the utmost sincerity, I do not think myself equal to the command I am honored with.

His chaplain in his diary shared recollections of how Washington found great comfort in Joshua chapter 1, and its encouragement about God's presence with him as he entered into battle.

Our minds are drawn to the events of 230 years ago, on this weekend when we celebrate the birth of our nation and the valor of those who gave their lives that we might be free. The "glorious Cause," in Washington's words, has also been fresh on the minds of millions today due to the tremendous popularity of historian David McCullough's number one best-seller this summer: *1776*. The book is a brilliant, highly-readable look at the opening days of the American War of Independence; it makes the key participants into real people—not patriotic saints on statues and monuments and in oil paintings on the White House walls, but normal folks who found themselves living in frightening, desperate times—people who had to make hard choices with no certainty of the outcome.

It seems appropriate to me that we think together for a few minutes about the lessons we can learn from those courageous people of the early days of our nation. History, when properly studied, should teach us not just facts and dates and events, but principles that can relate to our own lives. In fact, that's also how we need to study biblical history, the events recorded in the pages of Scripture. Though this may be a bit ambitious, what I want us to attempt to do today is to look at three principles for living, and examine each one from three separate angles: how it was demonstrated in the Bible, how it has been seen in American history, and how it relates to our own personal lives in the 21st century. This is a "three times three" message; I hope you'll be able to follow it, and I hope you will understand its application. Here are the three principles we will explore:

- God is active in human events.
- Nothing of great worth is achieved without struggle.
- God's blessings bring responsibilities.

God is active in human events.

This first principle is clear and unmistakable if we take the time to read the Book of Joshua in the Old Testament. Chapter 1 is the Prologue, filled with promises from God of success to come, as long as Joshua and his people will remain faithful and obedient. God intervenes in the course of events repeatedly: He causes the Jordan River to be blocked by a landslide long enough for the army to cross safely, then He knocks down the mighty walls of Jericho with a single breath. The conquest of the Promised Land has God's fingerprints all over it.

And I believe that God did not stop being active in human events with the conclusion of the Bible. He continues to intervene. Here is a trivia question for you: What is the final word of McCullough's book *1776*? How does it end? The final word is "miracle." This secular historian, though not professing a personal faith in the God of the Bible, uses a word with a very biblical meaning. What is a "miracle"? It is a direct intervention of God in human events. If even David McCullough can find no other explanation for the against-all-odds victory of the ragtag American army over the world's greatest superpower, how much more confident can Christians be in seeing God's fingerprints in the birth of our nation.

Let me give one example from that crucial year of 1776. It's been called by historians "The Battle of Brooklyn." A vastly superior force of British troops and ships had the Continental Army trapped on the western heights of Brooklyn on Long Island, their backs to the East River. Their only hope for escape would be to ferry 9,000 men across to Manhattan, but the risks were great. The Royal Navy warships in the harbor could blow the boats out of the water, while the British troops could overrun their trenches and bayonet them while they tried to retreat. It looked hopeless. But on the night of August 29, 1776, Washington prayed and then gave the order to evacuate. And then a series of events occurred that were so remarkable, every observer on both sides of the line commented on them. A howling "northeaster" storm began at dusk; the wind blew in exactly the direction required to keep the navy warships from being able to sail into the river. Hour after hour the small boats, loaded with weary American troops, made the crossing to Manhattan. Then, at dawn, with only half of the patriots safely evacuated, the rain stopped and an eerie fog appeared—as thick as any ever seen. It hung over Brooklyn and the East River for several hours, making it impossible for the British to see what the Americans were up to. Only as the final boat made it safely across did the fog lift. McCullough writes of this miracle:

> The immediate reaction of the British was ... one of utter astonishment. That the rebel army had silently vanished in the night under their very noses was almost inconceivable.[1]

Washington himself later wrote:

> The hand of Providence [that is, a direct intervention of God] has been so conspicuous in all this, that anyone who lacks faith must be worse than an infidel.

In many other incidents throughout our nation's history, we see that things happen beyond "coincidence." God can and does step in to the activities of human beings.

And He is active in our own lives today. Miracles do still happen. Some of you here today are walking medical miracles—you weren't supposed to make it. Some of you have seen the power of answered prayers in healing a broken marriage—or in healing you and putting you back together after you've lost a partner to death or divorce. Some of you have been able by God's power within you to break an addiction to alcohol. Some of you could give testimony today that it was only by God's grace that you have found forgiveness for your guilty conscience, and a new purpose for living. If you are in some difficult spot right now, don't stop praying and seeking the Lord and trusting Him, my friends. God is still at work among us!

Nothing of great worth is achieved without struggle.

This principle is seen clearly in the Book of Joshua. When God led His people to their Promised Land, He did not wipe out the pagan enemies there with a hurricane or earthquake. Instead, He sent Joshua and the troops to do the job. There was hard work, and hard fighting to do. And some of the Israeli troops had to be wounded and even die for the sake of the cause. All through scripture we find the same thing: when God calls His people to undertake a worthwhile goal, He prepares them for the cost. The supreme example in scripture, of course, is the death of our Savior on the cross. The greatest good imaginable for the entire human race could only be achieved through His indescribable suffering. So I think it's safe to say that if even the Son of God was not exempt from this requirement—that anything of great worth must be gained through struggle—then it is naive and foolish for you and me to think that we should get an easy, problem-free, pass through life!

The existence of our nation, the world's first true modern representative democracy, with its Constitution and Bill of Rights that have served as models and beacons of hope for oppressed people and newly-born nations around the globe over the past two centuries—this great nation of ours was born in struggle and suffering. If you're reading McCullough's book, you will be struck over and over with how difficult and desperate it was. John Adams wrote to his wife Abigail on July 4, 1776 these prophetic words:

> I am well aware of the toil and blood and treasure it will cost to maintain this Declaration, and support and defend these States. Yet through all the gloom I can see the rays of ravishing light and glory. I can see that the end is worth more than all the means.

The patriot and soldier Thomas Paine wrote these famous and gripping thoughts after yet another defeat by the British in 1776:

These are the times that try men's souls. The summer soldier and the sunshine patriot will, in this crisis, shrink from the service of his country; but he that stands it now, deserves the love and thanks of man and woman. Tyranny, like hell, is not easily conquered; yet we have this consolation with us, that the harder the conflict, the more glorious the triumph.

And what about for us today? Do we not also see confirmed, throughout our own lives, that the things of greatest value are the things that cost us the most to achieve? Many of us here have invested our lives in building a successful business, in raising God-fearing and successful children, in serving God and our church and community faithfully, in resisting temptation, in developing a prayer life. Are any of these easy? Of course not! They take everything we've got, and more. They require that we trust in God and draw upon His strength, just as Joshua and George Washington had to do daily. And they're worth it all. If you're feeling discouraged this morning because life is hard work, listen again to God's words to us: "I will never leave you or forsake you ... be strong and courageous ... do not be terrified or discouraged, for the LORD your God will be with you wherever you go."

God's blessings bring responsibilities.
This final principle is one we need to be reminded of constantly—for any people who are blessed by God will experience two powerful temptations: the temptation to take those blessings and hoard them for ourselves alone, and the temptation to think that our success has come by our own strength and cleverness.

When we fall into these blunders, we forget God's unmistakable teaching: (1) that He blesses us precisely so that we can be a blessing to others, can do His work in this world; and (2) that His blessings are always from Him alone, not by our own efforts, and that He expects us to be grateful and give Him the praise He is due.

In the up-and-down, roller-coaster experience of the people of Israel in the Old Testament we find that repeatedly, one generation after another, those men and women fell into the common mistakes. Whenever they failed to live out their purpose as holy people and examples to the other nations, they fell into hard times. Whenever they forgot about God and trusted only in themselves, they experienced the consequences. This is why, in His words of encouragement to Joshua, the Lord also spells out the responsibilities we have to obey Him and His word, to live righteous and holy lives: "Be careful to obey all the law … that you may be successful wherever you go" (Joshua 1:7).

This weekend is our nation's 229th birthday—which we celebrate on July 4, even though actually the Declaration was adopted in Congress on July 2, was written up by somebody with good penmanship on July 3 and then signed by the delegates with their "John Hancocks" the following day. It's nice to sing "Happy Birthday to us" and pat ourselves on the back. But I believe that we need to take very seriously God's commands to our nation. He has blessed us, but not for the ultimate purpose that we just get rich and happy. We have a place in world history. Just as we were each individually made for a purpose (as many of us were reminded in reading *The Purpose Driven Life*, by Rick Warren), so God allowed and intervened in the birth of the United States of America for a purpose.

We are called as a nation to be a force for freedom, for human rights, and for morality in this world. Our military might must be used for the right causes only—but it has not always been. Our media and our popular culture are witnessed around the globe—and often portray us and our morality in a shameful way. Our laws were intended by our Founding Fathers to follow principles of natural and biblical law—the ones Joshua was commanded so long ago to follow—yet many in our nation would have us turn our back on those timeless principles. Wealth is given to individuals and corporations to be shared with their workers and communities—yet greedy CEO's are grabbing for far more than they could ever possibly need or spend.

While we celebrate our nation's birth and heritage today, it is right that we call our country and its leaders to stay true to our founding principles, to recognize our purposes in the world, to be humble and grateful to God, and to follow His principles for nations. I believe we can love our nation and call it to greater faithfulness. In fact, that is the most loving thing we can do for our country: to be bold and faithful witnesses whenever America sins and strays from God's ways.

And each of us has a responsibility before God to respond to His blessings in the right way. Some of us have been blessed immensely in material comforts and assets—and yet we give back to the Lord and to others in need a pathetically small percentage, hoarding far more than necessary. Some of us are too stingy in hoarding our time and our energy, failing to give a fair part of ourselves in service to the Lord and others. Some of us have let our own personal discipline, our spiritual lives, and our relationships with our spouse become neglected. Some of us worship God on Sundays and then live the rest of the week as if He were a billion miles away. We need to be called back repeatedly to our purpose, to our allegiance to our Lord. We need to obey Him and allow ourselves to be a blessing to others in His name.

We have covered a lot of ground together. We have looked at three truths, and how they are demonstrated in biblical history, in American history, and in our personal lives. The message of scripture is true and relevant to all times and generations. May we be found faithful in our own days, as were our spiritual ancestors under Joshua's command, and our national ancestors under Washington!

Piloting a Flagship

October 29, 2006

In this message, Pastor Pratt unveiled the mission and vision
for First Church and issued a call to excellence.

Most Sundays we focus our thought and attention on God's Word in order to apply it to our own personal lives. And that's our primary purpose here; it's why most of us come on Sunday mornings: to get the Word from the Lord, to receive strength and guidance and encouragement to live as Christians amidst the challenges of daily life. But occasionally we need to devote a Sunday morning to reflecting on how God wants us to live corporately, rather than individually—as a church, a Christian family, rather than just as solo believers. He has made it very clear in Scripture, after all, that a "Lone Ranger Christian"—a self-sufficient and detached follower of Christ—is an oxymoron, a contradiction. We belong to one another. And it matters very much to the Lord how we function as His church.

Our study of God's Word today will be primarily derived from the wisdom of the Apostle Paul, the greatest apostle of the First Century Church. He was a pastor, an evangelist, an elder, a statesman, a visionary and a dynamic leader, all in one. God used Paul to not only guide the early days of the church, but to provide us with wisdom in his New Testament letters that applies equally to our own day.

But before we look at that, let me just remind you of a statement of Jesus—made to His followers and to us—recorded in Luke chapter 12. These words always convict me and cause me to catch my breath. They are profound and weighty. Here's what our Lord says to us: "From everyone who has been given much, much will be demanded; and from the one who has been entrusted with much, much more will be asked."

Has God blessed us? Yes, He certainly has. We have phenomenal resources of talents and abilities, of finances, of education and life experiences within this congregation. There are few churches in the world that have as much as we do! I know I've been blessed personally beyond what I could have imagined. But God's blessings are not to be hoarded, they are to be shared. If we have been given much, our Lord expects us to do much with those blessings. For me, as a pastor and one of the leaders of a congregation, that means that I can never settle for being mediocre. I can never be content with offering God the leftovers. He deserves nothing less than the absolute best we can do for Him!

Now let's turn to Paul's first letter to the church in the city of Corinth. I'll be reading selections from chapter three—and as I do so, here's what I want you to watch for. Notice the "analogies" of the church that Paul uses. An analogy is a word picture, comparing something that's more abstract— such as the Christian Church—to something concrete and visible in our daily lives. Try to find the analogies the Apostle uses for the fellowship of people gathered together in the name of Jesus Christ.

⁶I planted the seed, Apollos watered it, but God made it grow. ... ⁸The man who plants and the man who waters have one purpose, and each will be rewarded according to his own labor. ⁹For we are God's fellow workers; you are God's field, God's building.

¹⁰By the grace God has given me, I laid a foundation as an expert builder, and someone else is building on it. But each one should be careful how he builds. ¹¹For no one can lay any foundation other than the one already laid, which is Jesus Christ. ...

¹⁶Don't you know that you yourselves are God's temple and that God's Spirit lives in you? – 1 CORINTHIANS 3:6-11, 16

Did you catch the ways in which Paul uses common images to help us understand the true nature of the church? He first describes it as a field or garden, with the leaders as gardeners working to bring forth nourishing fruit. Then, in verse 9, his mind switches to the image of a building; he and other leaders are the architects and bricklayers, and every member of the church is a separate building block, with Jesus as the concrete footer on which everything is anchored. Then, in verse 16, he throws in a new analogy: the church is like a great temple, a place of worship filled with the presence of God.

All of these analogies work, and yet each is just partial. In other places the New Testament describes the church as being like:

- a human body, with every part connected together and directed by the head, Christ;
- a family, with all Christians as brothers and sisters under God our common Heavenly Father;
- a grapevine, with each of us as branches bearing fruit as we are attached to the root of Christ.

With the multitude of biblical images available, I feel it's permissible to suggest another analogy that is specific to the calling and ministry our own congregation has within our sphere of influence and work here in southwest Florida. You will find in the Strategic Plan a vision for this congregation to serve as a "flagship" church for our community. I'd like to take a moment to explain that image—and what it does and does not mean to us. The term "flagship" derives from the days when great navies roamed the seven seas. A flagship was the ship of the fleet's admiral, and it was usually the strongest ship, the one that went first into battle to show the way for others. Today the term flagship has become common in the business world. For many years—until it was bought by a big national corporation that changed its name—the great Marshall Field's department store was the trendsetter for the Chicago area. And the flagship store on Michigan Avenue was renowned worldwide as a center for excellence in retailing—the place where store managers for the suburban satellite stores were trained, the place where the leading merchandise was tested. For many years the great General Motors ruled the world of the automotive industry, and during those decades everyone recognized that the flagship brand was the great Cadillac—revered as the finest in quality and excellence and luxury.

What is a "flagship church"? It is a congregation that has been blessed by God with great resources—material resources and human resources (and, of course, as Jesus said, those who are blessed with much will be expected to do much in return). A flagship church is a congregation that is willing to pursue excellence, to offer itself as a role model and example to others, to take the lead in a community when the church needs to speak and to act for the cause of Christ. It's not easy to do this. And any church that presumes to be a flagship for its own ego and glory, rather than purely for the glory and honor of Jesus our Lord, will ultimately find itself disqualified from true glory; the only kind of leadership that works in the Kingdom of God is humble, selfless, "servant leadership." Being a flagship church does not obligate us to do everything—any more than the Marshall Field's flagship store felt it necessary to offer every item of merchandise in the world. But whatever we determine to do, we must do well, to the best of our human and God-inspired ability.

The Strategic Plan your Elders have written and adopted as our vision for the years to come lays out this challenging goal for us. We believe that we have a unique opportunity, and are uniquely-positioned within this area, to really make a difference. We are not only by far the largest Protestant and Evangelical church in Bonita Springs, and one of the largest Presbyterian churches in all of southern Florida; we also are blessed by literally thousands of people who worship with us for one Sunday or more who can take back the message that God has touched them with here to their own communities all around the United States and beyond—so that someone who hears the Word of God in one of our pews some Sunday may end up making a profound difference in a community or a corporation that we will never hear about. But God will know.

My purpose for the final few minutes we have this morning is to help you understand where we believe the Lord wants our church to go in the years immediately ahead of us. In all human endeavors a key factor is the character of leadership. Who are the leaders—the captains and lieutenants of this flagship—and what are they like? I feel it's important that I tell you a bit about myself and the other pastors, the staff and the elected elders whom God has put into positions of responsibility for this ship. It's not that it's all about me or us, by any means; a church does not exist for its pastors and elders, but rather they exist for the purpose of serving the church. But inevitably a congregation takes on and reflects something of the faith, the values, the ethics, the personalities and the style of its leaders.

Here's what you need to know about me and the other leaders of this flagship as we sail into an unknown future.

We are unanimously and passionately committed to preserving and proclaiming the historic and biblical faith. In that sense we are traditionalists or conservatives of the most profound kind: what God has given to us we must protect and cherish, rather than change. We all know that the Christian faith is under open attack today not only from those outside the church (be they radical Islamists or atheists in the news media and entertainment industry and college campuses); our faith is also being attacked from within, by ministers and priests and seminary professors and scholars whose beliefs and philosophies and lifestyles are directly contrary to the teachings of Scripture. But we want you to know that everything we do in this church will be faithful to the Bible—from our sermons and worship services to our Bible studies, our children's classes and youth groups, our Great Banquet renewal weekends and mission projects. We believe with all our hearts that it is not our place to stand in judgment over the Bible, deciding which parts we'll believe and follow and which parts we'll dismiss. Rather, we are convinced that God's Word stands in judgment over us, as Truth to be received and obeyed.

We will focus our energies entirely on spiritual growth and practical service within our congregation and to our community and world. It is not our calling to be involved directly in politics. I have never, and I will never, endorse a party or candidate from the pulpit. I'll be happy to share with you privately my own viewpoints and listen with respect to yours. But we will not let our church be sidetracked from its mission into partisan politics.

And this is true not only for secular politics, but for church and denominational politics as well. I've put in my time with denominational struggles, and it's not my calling now. I am devoted 100% to this congregation and its ministry. I and our pastoral staff and Session are uncompromising in where we stand and what we believe, but we choose to not dilute our energies from our primary calling by getting caught up in intramural squabbles within the Presbyterian denomination. Church fights can suck the life and spirit out of a congregation. Our mission to be a "flagship" is too important to let that happen.

We're in this for the long haul. I can't speak for the other staff, but only for myself in this respect. God has called me to be your pastor for the rest of my full-time ministry, until my retirement at 65 (or 68 or 70 or whatever). I'm not going anywhere, no matter what openings arise in any pulpit in America. I'm not interested, and I'm not available. This is my home, and you are my family.

That's enough about me. Let me direct your attention to our Mission Statement, which is printed on the back of our bulletin every week. This is what God has called us to do. Do you recall how, 12 years ago, the Republican leadership in Congress put forth an agenda or Strategic Plan that they called "The Contract with America"? Newt Gingrich and the other GOP leaders laid out their hopes for the future, and on that basis they asked for the support of the American electorate, who put them into power. Though we may argue with whether that party has delivered on its promise, the principle is a sound one: it's only appropriate to ask people for their support if you first make clear what you intend to do. So here, following the order in our Mission Statement, is what we pledge to provide at this church in the years to come.

PART ONE: *To be a welcoming and nurturing family.* We offer to you a place for friendship and support. All of us at times in life have special needs. We may have a problem with our health, the loss of a loved one, or personal or family problems. There are many supports available: doctors, dentists, lawyers, counselors and neighbors. But we offer you a place to find Christian and spiritual support. And we believe that this is something everyone needs and longs for. We also offer a place for acceptance and belonging around the core values of the Christian faith. There are many opportunities for social interaction and recreation and entertainment in our community. They're all good, and they all have a place. But we can offer something as a church that you don't find at a country club, a service club, the Art League, the Philharmonic, the YMCA or the shopping mall. You need to be a part of a welcoming and nurturing church.

PART TWO: *To help people grow as followers of Jesus Christ.* If you will come and participate and put yourself into the worship experiences we provide weekly, you will get to know God better and grow in your faith and understanding. The messages will be both biblical and practical, relating the ancient faith to the realities of modern life. The music and the other elements of the service will be of high quality, open and accessible to people of all church backgrounds and experiences. As a complement to our weekly gatherings for worship, we will provide a wide range of other opportunities for you to grow and be equipped to live your faith. As long as we still have minds that are alert, we can grow in our knowledge of God and our relationship with Him. We are a people who are excited about being lifelong learners.

PART THREE: *To make a positive difference in today's world.* All of us have a need to know that our lives count for something. God created in us this longing for significance. And every Christian has been given gifts and talents by the Lord to use for His glory and to help and serve others. Whether your gift is best used within the church or in the community, we will offer repeated encouragement and help and motivation to you to find where you can make a positive difference for someone else.

Those are the things we pledge to you. If this is what you're looking for in a church, we pray that you will come and be with us whenever you can, participate in the financial support of the church as God has enriched and blessed you, and invite your friends, neighbors and co-workers to come try us out.

That is my message to you today: a promise of what this church will aspire to be and do, and an invitation to each of you to be part of it. It's a call to the pursuit of excellence in our Christian lives. Pursuing excellence is never easy, and it's always costly. It's also the most exciting and fulfilling way to live.

Imagine a group of hikers in the gorgeous Yosemite National Park in California. Most of them decide to take it easy, to enjoy a leisurely stroll through the meadows and along the paths lying in the valley. But a few of them decide to leave their backpacks and their friends behind and scale the cliffs. The ascent is hard, and wearying, and it takes all they've got. At times the going is slow and dangerous. But those few travelers who are not content with the easy way are rewarded in the end. By choosing to pay the price to climb to the heights, they receive a breathtaking view that is like nothing available to those who remain in the comfort and security of the valley below.

I don't know about you, but I want to be a climber, not just a casual stroller. I want my life to count for something, and I want to be part of a church that's not content with the mediocre. Together, by God's grace and His Spirit within us, if we commit ourselves to the pursuit of excellence, we will experience things that we could never otherwise imagine. And who wouldn't want to devote their time and treasure, their energies and emotions, to something that great?

Closing the Loophole

JUNE 24, 2007

God's word is timeless and timely. In this message, Pastor Pratt demonstrated how the parables of Jesus can guide us in responding to issues of our day.

Jesus replied, "A man was going down from Jerusalem to Jericho, and fell into the hands of robbers, who stripped him, beat him, and went away, leaving him half dead. ³¹Now by chance a priest was going down that road; and when he saw him, he passed by on the other side. ³²So likewise a Levite, when he came to the place and saw him, passed by on the other side. ³³But a Samaritan while traveling came near him; and when he saw him he was moved with pity. ³⁴He went to him and bandaged his wounds, having poured oil and wine on them. Then he put him on his own animal, brought him to an inn, and took care of him. ³⁵The next day he took out two denarii, gave them to the innkeeper, and said, 'Take care of him; and when I come back, I will repay you whatever more you spend.' ³⁶Which of these three, do you think, was a neighbor to the man who fell into the hands of the robbers?" ³⁷He said, "The one who showed him mercy." Jesus said to him, "Go and do likewise."
– LUKE 10:30-37 (NRSV)

*T*his is probably the most widely-known and famous of all the stories and parables Jesus told. Everyone knows about the "Good Samaritan"; states and countries have "Good Samaritan Laws" on the books to protect those who offer help; an organization of RV and camping enthusiasts who are dedicated to providing roadside assistance has named itself "The Good Sam Club." Everybody knows the story of the foreigner who stepped in to help when the religious professionals of this poor crime victim's own people ignored him.

There are actually two categories of people who emerge from this story smelling a bit like rotten fish. One of them is my own, the clergy. The Priest and the Levite were too busy, and too concerned about their ceremonial purity, and too steeped in their own snobbery and pride, to get their hands dirty. But there is one other profession that likewise takes its lumps in this chapter of scripture; and to see this we need to back up a bit and study the Parable of the Good Samaritan in its context. Let's read the verses immediately preceding it.

²⁵Just then a lawyer stood up to test Jesus. "Teacher," he said, "what must I do to inherit eternal life?" ²⁶[Jesus] said to him, "What is written in the law? What do you read there?" ²⁷He answered, "You shall love the Lord your God with all your heart, and with all your soul, and with all your strength, and with all your mind; and your neighbor as yourself." ²⁸And He said to him, "You have given the right answer; do this, and you will live."

²⁹But wanting to justify himself, he asked Jesus, "And who is my neighbor?" ³⁰Jesus replied, "A man was going down from Jerusalem to Jericho, and fell into the hands of robbers …" – LUKE 10:25-30 (NRSV)

The Parable of the Good Samaritan was birthed in the context of a lawyer looking for a loophole. Now I want to make it clear that I am not attempting to smear or slander an entire profession. There are some lawyers and retired lawyers here among us. I promise you that I will not be engaging in the usual "lawyer jokes" (though I do know some pretty funny ones). I have personally known many legal professionals in the congregations I've served who are people of upright and unimpeachable character.

But in this particular case, it was a lawyer who was caught trying to weasel his way out of the requirements of scripture. And it's not really surprising that a lawyer would be looking for a loophole in the law, for, of course, the law is their business, their primary focus; lawyers are supposed to know the law backward and forward, inside and out. But this particular attorney was trying to find a loophole that didn't exist—and Jesus caught him in the act and set him straight.

What does the Parable of the Good Samaritan teach us? Its clear message is that all human beings—no matter their differences in race, nationality, culture, language, education, wealth and social standing—are all equal in the eyes of God. The command to "love our neighbor as [we love] ourselves" is a very high bar, the ultimate ethical standard.

The "loophole" the lawyer was desperately looking for was in the area of defining who is a "neighbor"? Do you remember when a prominent politician a decade ago was caught doing something wrong, and tried to find a loophole by quibbling over definitions: "It depends on what the meaning of the word 'is' is." That's what the man who came to Jesus was trying to do: *If I can just define "neighbor" in the right and convenient way, then maybe I can claim to be innocent according to the strict letter of the law.* But Jesus slams that loophole shut. He tells us that if a person we meet or know has a need, and we can help to meet that need, then that person is our neighbor—and therefore we are commanded to offer love to them in practical ways.

That's the simple and direct teaching of scripture. If it doesn't touch each of our hearts and consciences, we are simply not listening. But I want to take a step further, and venture into some controversial and dangerous territory in our final few minutes today. I want to try to apply this teaching of our Lord to one of the important moral and ethical issues of our time.

This issue has also become a political hot potato. Now it is my policy to never endorse a particular political party or candidate as part of any message I bring in a worship service. While I always vote, and belong to a party, and have my own personal views, when I speak as your pastor I attempt to be non-partisan and objective.

The issue I want us to think about is the complex problem of immigration—its laws and their enforcement in America today. This has become highly politicized by a proposal in our Congress that keeps getting debated and changed and amended—a proposal that is highly controversial. I haven't read the total bill, but I've been reading lots of analyses from both the left and the right—and almost every article and op-ed piece and speech causes me to nod my head: "Yes, I agree with those points." Apparently everybody finds something in the proposed legislation they like, and at least one or more things that they hate. I am not smart enough to know if the current plan will work or not. But there are certain basic principles I sense most of us could agree upon: We all want to see our borders secure and protected; we want to see the laws of our country upheld, not ignored or un-enforced; and we believe in the principle that all people who work should pay their taxes, and that there should be a balance between what immigrants contribute to our country and what they receive in services from it. These are sound and sensible values.

What we need to be careful about is that, in upholding our national laws and security, we not fall into false and unbiblical attitudes towards our newest immigrants. We must not look upon them all as evil criminals, nor as less-than-human beasts of burden, nor as threats to our way of life. The issues of immigration and assimilation are not new, of course. They've existed as long as America has been settled. Your ancestors and mine were immigrants to this country. Some arrived with a deed in their pockets from a distant king—though his authority wasn't recognized by the Native Americans whose land they wanted to take. Some of our ancestors came in chains as slaves or indentured servants. Some came as refugees from famine or oppression or political persecution in their homeland. Many of our ancestors, when they arrived here—from Sicily or Poland or Sweden or Korea or Nigeria—were just as uneducated and penniless and unable to speak English as the newest arrival yesterday in Immokalee. Many of them faced mistrust and persecution from those who were already settled in America. Our nation's history has seen previous waves of sentiment to "seal the borders" and "ship them all back home." But we haven't done that. And over time, with the great "melting pot" of our culture, as the first generation is succeeded by the second and third, the immigrants become true Americans—and our nation is stronger and better because of them.

Whatever political and legal changes our country's leadership ultimately decides to take, I want to keep the focus local. This is not just a problem we can leave in the laps of "those people" in Washington. What about us as individuals living in Southwest Florida … and what about us as a church? What is Jesus calling us to do?

We have to begin by confessing that the problems and needs of this world are too vast and too complex and too overwhelming for any of us to solve. If we truly open our eyes to the full spectrum of human needs in Immokalee and the migrant camps in central Florida, or the needs in the inner cities across America, or the needs in poverty-stricken Africa, or the needs in the violence-torn Middle East, it could cause us to give up in frustration. But that doesn't do any good … and it's not God's will for us to feel hopeless. I believe that there are a few things—let's call them "Principles for Modern Good Samaritans"—we need to do to become useful to the Lord and effective in fulfilling the command to "love our neighbor as ourselves" in the midst of a world of vast problems.

Principle #1: Let God lead us individually and personally.

Since none of us can do it all, we need to allow God to touch our heart with the one thing or two things He wants us to do. What touches your conscience may be different from what touches mine. That's okay. It's how the Holy Spirit works. None of us have unlimited resources or time or ability, but we all can do something.

Principle #2: Work in partnership.

We can accomplish more by working with like-minded people than we can alone. I am excited by the way the churches, nonprofits, city government and businesses of our community have been feeling the nudge to start working together more closely. And I am hopeful that in the coming days and months you'll be seeing and reading in our local papers about more ways we can partner together.

Principle #3: Love people holistically.

That means that we recognize how God created us. We are not just bodies who need food and health care and shelter. We are not just minds who need education and literacy. We are not just economic machines that need jobs and money. We are whole people. All of these needs are interconnected. And we all live in families and communities that impact us in multiple ways. To see people holistically is to recognize the multiple dimensions of life. God loves each person in their body, their mind, their relationships and their soul.

Principle #4: Help direct each person to their Heavenly Father.

This final principle is directly related to the previous one. As we begin to recognize the multiple dimensions of a person's life, we find that the spiritual dimension is often neglected—but what a difference it makes! We see this on foreign mission fields: When a people who have been living in spiritual darkness, without a relationship to God, come to know Him through Jesus the Savior and begin to learn His Word, every aspect of life changes. People stop drinking and living only for pleasure, and become hard-working and productive people who take care of themselves. Their economic conditions thus change. They start living in fidelity to their marriages and caring for their families. They stop breaking laws and become obedient citizens. Entire communities have been transformed by the Gospel.

When social service organizations and foundations try to treat only one aspect of a community—for example, the sanitation, the health care, the education, the economy—without touching other areas, those efforts frequently fail to bear fruit. Why? Because human beings have moral and spiritual dimensions as well as physical and economic.

We are committed as a church to providing a variety of holistic ministries to touch the various needs of individuals in our community and area, as well as in other countries. But we want those efforts to always have a spiritual dimension to them. That's why we are investing to help start a church in Immokalee. If we, a Christian congregation, don't help to begin new churches, no one else will. The State of Florida won't. The United Way won't. This is a part that we uniquely can do. Only churches can "birth" other churches.

And the culture of immigrant communities across the U.S. indicates that planting new churches is a very successful strategy. When people come together in the love of Christ, they become a true, spiritual, supportive community. Other ministries, to their physical and economic needs, can flow naturally out of a church's life and outreach. And in communities like Immokalee, planting a number of smaller 100- and 200-member churches is a better strategy than trying to create another "First Presbyterian" with a couple thousand people. In our community and culture a big church like this works well; in other cultures, smaller churches are more effective—

because they can operate as large extended families.

We've been trying to look honestly, without excuses or loopholes, at the eternally challenging Parable of the Good Samaritan and the piercing words of Jesus. It is my prayer that we as individual Christians and as a church will grow more sensitive in our consciences to the promptings of our Lord: to recognize our neighbor, to see his or her needs, and to feel the promptings of the Holy Spirit to know what we can do to help.

The Dying Captain's Final Words

MARCH 2, 2008

Committed to using the most effective means for sharing God's truth,
Pastor Pratt's messages are enhanced by a variety of audio-visuals.
The story that serves as the primary illustration in this sermon
was actually shared in the form of a film clip.

A Great Sacrifice

One of the most dramatic and moving films about human conflict ever made is Steven Spielberg's *Saving Private Ryan*. Millions of viewers have watched the closing credits of that movie through a film of tears, powerfully touched by its message. Thousands of veterans of the Second World War and other conflicts have found that the vivid scenes of combat and military life helped unlock years of hidden memories within them.

The film tells the story of U.S. Infantry Captain John Miller (played by Tom Hanks). After surviving the hellish first-wave assault on Omaha Beach on D-Day, Miller and his squad are given a bizarre assignment. They are ordered on a wild goose chase through Nazi-occupied Normandy to find a U.S. paratrooper named Private James Ryan. The Pentagon has ordered this unprecedented move because Ryan's three older brothers, all fighting in the war, have recently been killed in various actions around the globe. For P.R. purposes, the top brass have decided to rescue Private Ryan from the heat of battle, bring him home, discharge him and return him to his family in Iowa. The lot falls to Captain Miller to try to find this "needle in a stack of needles" and bring him back alive.

Finally the private is located. But before Captain Miller can get him back to Omaha Beach for evacuation, they find themselves in the middle of a vicious firefight with counterattacking Germans. In the battle for a strategic bridge, Captain Miller is mortally wounded. When reinforcements arrive to drive the Germans back, Private Ryan bends over to his rescuer. And Captain Miller, with his last breath, grabs Private Ryan by the shirt and pleads with him, "Earn this. Earn it." Those are words that James Ryan can never forget.

At the end of the film, former Private Ryan returns some 50 years later to the U.S. military cemetery in Normandy, with his wife and children and grandchildren by his side. He searches among the rows of thousands of white crosses, until he finds Captain Miller's grave. Ryan breaks down in tears before the cross that stands above the man who gave his life to save Ryan's. He turns to his wife. "Tell me I've been a good man," he implores her. It's clear that this man, James Ryan, once a young private and now an aging grandfather, has lived the past 50 years cherishing the memory of his deliverer, John Miller, and hoping to live in a way that is worthy of that great sacrifice. Captain Miller gave his life to save Private Ryan, and Ryan knows that he owes everything he has and everything he is to that sacrificial act.

The Greatest Sacrifice

Whenever a group of Christians gather together for worship, what we are really doing is remembering and commemorating a sacrifice that was even greater and more moving than the one made by Captain Miller to rescue Private Ryan. In a high-stakes cosmic battle for our souls, our great Rescuer gave His life for every one of us. His death isn't just signified by a cross standing in a cemetery, like Captain Miller's. No, it actually happened on a cross. And these are the words written by a man named Paul, reflecting on the significance of that death.

You see, at just the right time, when we were still powerless, Christ died for the ungodly. ⁷Very rarely will anyone die for a righteous man, though for a good man someone might possibly dare to die. ⁸But God demonstrates His own love for us in this: While we were still sinners, Christ died for us. ⁹Since we have now been justified by His blood, how much more shall we be saved from God's wrath through Him! – Romans 5:6-9

There are two important characteristics we need to understand about a Great Sacrifice, such as that of Captain Miller for Private Ryan, or that of Jesus our Savior for the entire human race. A sacrifice like this cannot be earned and cannot be reimbursed.

A Great Sacrifice Cannot Be Earned

When we earn something, we work for it and then are given a paycheck upon completion of that service. Earning is what we do prior to compensation. A transaction that occurs before any work is done, or apart from any merit on our parts, is a gift. A gift is granted without being earned. This distinction is very important to grasp. Technically there is no way we can ever "earn" the sacrifice of another person dying in our place—let alone that of God Himself, our Creator and Lord.

Paul makes it clear that this is especially true in relation to the sacrifice of Christ. None of us could ever claim that we're entirely good, perfect people. The undeniable fact of human existence is that every one of us is an imperfect, flawed sinner. We've all disobeyed God and in our selfishness have wandered away from Him. There is absolutely no way that any of us could ever stand in Heaven's courtroom and try to press a claim against God, as if He owed you or me anything.

In the climactic scene of the Spielberg film, Captain Miller did say to Private Ryan, "Earn this." But we can certainly forgive that dying officer for making a semantic mistake. In actual fact Private Ryan could not possible "earn" his deliverance. It was a gift, pure and simple. And whatever else James Ryan does for the rest of his life, he is not "earning" what he received from Captain Miller—because the gift had already been given in full. Earning is what we do before a wage is paid to us. But the Captain has paid everything in advance.

A Great Sacrifice Cannot Be Reimbursed

It is simply impossible to compensate someone for the Ultimate Sacrifice. Private Ryan cannot repay Captain Miller by giving the Captain his life back. It's impossible—the clock cannot be turned backwards. And in a far greater sense, you and I can never repay or reimburse Jesus for what He suffered on the cross to save us. All the good deeds we could ever do for the rest of our lives couldn't come close to settling the account. In fact, not a single person has ever gotten to the place where they could claim to be "all square" with God, having given to Him just as much as He has given to them. There is not a chance—His gifts are far greater than we could ever reimburse or repay.

What We Can Do With a Great Sacrifice

So what are we to do with such a costly, precious gift? How can we cope with such a great sacrifice offered for us? I believe there are three natural and appropriate responses.

1. We can receive the Great Gift. We accept it humbly, in gratitude and thankfulness. It was hard for Private Ryan, when Captain Miller first informed him that he was going home, to accept his deliverance. He thought he should stay with his airborne division in the field—that is what he had been trained and equipped to do. Going home so soon seemed wrong to him—so humbling, such a blow to his macho pride. In the same way, many men and women have initially rejected the gracious gift Jesus offers to them. Psychologically it can be difficult to accept a gift, especially if doing so means that we need to admit we're not perfect, that we need help and forgiveness, as is required in accepting the gift of Jesus. But this first step of consciously, willfully and intentionally receiving the gift of God's grace is so essential.

Some people have the misguided idea that if Christ died on the cross for the sins of all mankind, then that forgiveness is automatically applied to everyone, whether they want it or not. The gift is yours, so the twisted thinking goes, even if you don't receive it. That mistake can be eternally deadly for those who make it.

A few years ago a major class action lawsuit was won against a large corporation by a plaintiff's attorney. The verdict, ordering the company to reimburse all the people who had bought a defective product, theoretically applied to everyone. But each person was required by the judge's ruling to individually apply to the company for their refund before it was granted. Even though the hard part—the grueling court battle—had been won for them by the attorney, every person who was party to the class action still had to do their part. They had to ask and receive. They had to put in writing their desire that the benefits of the victory be applied to them. They had to request their refund check, and only when they did so would it be issued to them. Was the judge in the case unjust or cruel in laying down this simple requirement? I don't think so.

The exact same principle is found in the spiritual realm. Jesus has won the class action battle on behalf of all of us. The payoff—forgiveness of our sins and eternal life—is waiting for us; it's ours simply for the asking. But until we individually ask the Great Judge to credit the result of this great victory won on the cross to our account, it's not yet ours.

2. We can remember the Giver—honoring His name and His memory. I suspect that not a day passed for 50 years of James Ryan's life that he did not think about Captain Miller's sacrifice for him. And if anyone should dare to say anything negative about John Miller in his presence, don't you think Ryan would rise up in righteous indignation and protest: "Don't talk about that man like that. He gave his life for me!" We Christians, who have been saved by the sacrifice of Jesus, sometimes find ourselves in situations where people are using the name of our Redeemer as a curse word. And we have every right to speak out in protest: "Please don't talk about my Lord like that. He gave His life for me!" I know it's easier to swallow our tongues and just go along to avoid confrontation. But, frankly, if we really love our Lord, we ought to be willing to take a little risk by speaking up to defend His name and His honor—especially after everything He risked for us!

3. We can respond—by living every day in such a way that our Redeemer would be proud of us. I'm sure that's what Captain Miller really meant to say to Private Ryan with his dying words: "Make me proud of you, James. Live your life the way I would, if I could live through you for the next 50 years."

And this is what Jesus asks of you and me. He knows we can never earn or deserve His love and grace and sacrifice. He doesn't ask us to try. What He does invite us to do is to become the kind of people of whom He can be proud. He wants us to follow His way, to love and serve others, just as He did during His earthly days. That's the way we demonstrate to Him that we really are grateful and appreciative of what He's done for us.

At the Foot of a Cross

Thinking often about the sacrifice of Christ can impact the way we look at all of life. At the end of this service we will sing the great hymn of our faith, *When I Survey the Wondrous Cross*. For nearly three centuries now these words have inspired Christians:

When I survey the wondrous cross,
on which the Prince of glory died
my richest gain I count but loss,
and pour contempt on all my pride.
Were the whole realm of nature mine,
that were a present far too small;
love so amazing, so divine,
demands my soul, my life, my all.

As James Ryan stood at the foot of a white cross in a Normandy cemetery, and examined his life in the light of the great sacrifice of his deliverer, so we stand this morning at the foot of the Cross of Jesus. The appropriate response of a grateful soul to a sacrifice such as this is to offer these words:

Lord Jesus, I believe you died for me.
I know I could never earn or repay your gift.
I now receive that gift.
I want to live for you and serve you.
I give you my soul, my life, my all.

If you're ready now to say this to Him—for the first time ever, or again as a rededication of your life—please join me as we pray…

Praising God When Life Stinks

FEBRUARY 22, 2009

*A voracious reader of wide interests, only our esteemed pastor
could find a way to blend the thoughts of C.S. Lewis
with the writings of Dr. Seuss in the same message!*

We would all love to be able to see into the future. Imagine that six
months ago we had been able to see what was about to happen. We would
have sold all our stocks and put our money in CDs and Treasuries. We
would have bet on the Phillies to win the World Series, the Gators to win
the college football championship, and the Steelers to win the Super Bowl.
Yes, we'd all love to know the future. Or would we? Do we really want to
know all the things that will happen to us and to those we love—even the
rotten, painful, frightening things? Or would that knowledge paralyze us?

A man with the funny name of Habakkuk, many centuries ago, actually was given by God a glimpse into his and his nation's future. And it was
not a pretty picture at all. In fact, things were about to become far worse
than they've been in America recently. His nation was about to enter a deep

and desperate economic recession, complicated by a disastrous military defeat and governmental turmoil. Things would quickly go from bad to worse to unbelievably awful.

But notice how this man Habakkuk responds to that word of warning from the Lord, as found in the closing verses of his self-titled book:

Though the fig tree does not bud and there are no grapes on the vines, though the olive crop fails and the fields produce no food, though there are no sheep in the pen and no cattle in the stalls, [18]yet I will rejoice in the LORD, I will be joyful in God my Savior. [19]The Sovereign LORD is my strength; he makes my feet like the feet of a deer, he enables me to go on the heights.
– *HABAKKUK 3:17-19*

It's amazing, isn't it? Though life for Habakkuk and his family and friends is about to become very hard, he chooses to still praise God and trust in Him. Those words, and the attitude and decision behind them, are going to stand as our example today.

A Common Assumption

Let's think for a moment about a common assumption held by a large number of people. The conventional wisdom of our day is that people are able to feel gratitude and happiness, and even to praise God, when things are going well for them personally. But when life stinks, when things are going badly—when one is in trouble, in pain, in debt—then it's impossible to praise God. That's what many people assume. We praise, we give thanks, and we rejoice when all is well, but we feel gloom and desperation when the chart of our fortunes turns south.

The reality, however, is something quite different. In fact, many people who find themselves in a season of prosperity and success are anything but grateful to God and brimming over with praise to Him. Success can simply make us proud, self-centered and blind to the spiritual world. And, in fact, many people who find themselves in hard situations are intensely close to the Lord, conscious of His presence in their lives, of His mercy and grace and sustaining power—even as they grapple with seemingly hopeless or insolvable problems.

We have a clever reminder of this paradox of life (that success does not automatically make us better, nor hardships automatically make us worse) in the pages of one of the classics of 20th century American children's literature. Lest you think I'm entering my second childhood of doddering old age and senility by talking about a simple children's book, let me remind you of the observation of none other than C.S. Lewis, one of the finest Christian authors and thinkers of all time. He often commented that the best in children's literature can be as profound and truthful as any adult literature, because it speaks of the principles of life without the complications and confusions of many adult-oriented stories.

Where do we find a children's story that tells us of the paradox of praising when life stinks? In Dr. Seuss's *How the Grinch Stole Christmas.* Theodore Geisel, a.k.a. Dr. Seuss, was a wise man—as generations of children and their parents have discovered. His books contain fairly sophisticated moral lessons. The tale of the Grinch is familiar to most of you. He lives on top of a mountain that overlooks the little town of Whoville. The Grinch, who is a miserable creature (one whose heart was "two sizes too small") despises the people of the town. They are always happy, always positive, always celebrating something. Of all days of the year, the Grinch has come to loathe Christmas the most. So one year he concocts a devilish plot. Late at night on Christmas Eve, he sneaks into the town and steals everything that has to do with Christmas: the gifts, the decorations and the food. He loads them all in his big sleigh and hauls them up to the top of Mount Crumpit. He is about to dump everything into the abyss when he notices that the sun is about to rise. He strains to hear the sounds of wailing and mourning from the town.

But, to his astonishment, the sound that rises to him at dawn is not one of grief but joy. The people of the town are singing Christmas carols. The Grinch can't understand it—he thought Christmas was all about things. Finally, Dr. Seuss tells us, "his heart grew three sizes that day." The moral of the story: joy and thankfulness are not determined by our outer circumstances. They come from within us.

The Biblical Understanding of Reality

If you won't trust Dr. Seuss to present the truth of human experience to you, will you trust the Word of God? Throughout scripture we are reminded of this important distinction between our situation and our response. Our friend Habakkuk is just one of numerous examples in the Bible of people who chose to follow a course of praise to God and trust in God in the midst of some pretty rotten circumstances.

We have people in this congregation today who are going through very difficult times. And no pious words or cheerful songs will change the reality of their financial squeeze, the disease afflicting their body with continual pain, the emptiness of a double bed each night with a spouse suddenly gone, the constant pressures of trying to raise a family and earn a living alone, or the stresses of trying to live like a Christian in a hostile corporate environment. Some of you came here today exhausted from the struggles of the past week, knowing that another week of pressures just like the last is waiting for you.

How do we get ourselves into such situations? There are a variety of reasons, of course. Sometimes life is difficult because of choices we've made, mistakes with consequences we've brought on ourselves. In situations like that, blaming God or feeling self-pity does no good. The smart thing to do is always to come back to the Lord—repenting and acknowledging our mistakes if we need to. Praising God when we're boiling in a stew of our own recipe is a way to bring humility, insight and perspective to us—and it helps us find the right way out of our mess.

Sometimes life is difficult because of forces and factors beyond our control. None of us is self-sufficient, able to manipulate everything and everyone in our environment for our own pleasure. Sometimes people treat us badly, or accidents happen, and we have to deal with them through our faith and God's strength.

And sometimes our problems and difficulties can actually be a gift from God. I know this sounds like heresy to us modern Americans, who have become addicted to comfort, health and prosperity. But the Bible makes it very clear that God can bring hardships to us for the purpose of teaching us things and developing strength of character and maturity within us that we would never otherwise learn. This is the case with Habakkuk and the people of God in the Old Testament: it was a part of God's plan for them—a plan for good, for ultimate blessing and redemption. I have watched many people go through tough ordeals in their own life or that of a family member, and they have grown spiritually through those experiences, coming out wiser and stronger on the other side.

So if we can agree that life, at times, is difficult, let's now consider our response to such situations. Why and how should we praise God?

Why Should We Praise God?

First, we should praise God because we always have blessings from the Lord's hand that we don't deserve, and therefore we always have something for which to be grateful and thankful. Everyone who is alive can thank God for that moment's breath—for, indeed, it is the power of God that upholds and sustains us every moment of our earthly existence. And everyone who has trusted in Jesus Christ can thank God in the moment of their final breath that their place in heaven for all eternity is secure, through the saving grace and mercy of our Lord. Counting our blessings and remembering all the things we may unconsciously take for granted is a theme we often hear at Thanksgiving time. But it's something we can and should do every day of the year—not just on a Thursday in November, wedged in between the turkey and the football.

Second, we should praise God because He is with us and is working in us in the hard times as well as the good times. You and I are not always aware of how we're growing and changing as it's happening to us—any more than a teenager is aware of his or her daily growth, as they are transformed before our eyes from children to young adults. If you are regularly praising and worshipping God and sharing your life with Him, you are growing. And remember: our Lord's ultimate purpose for you and me is not happiness but holiness—He wants us to become like His Son Jesus.

The third reason why we should praise God is because doing so regularly "refuels our tanks" and strengthens us for the next lap in life's journey. Like the pit stops that race car drivers take to get gas and fresh tires, so we need to pull into our "pit" here at church, and let our Supreme Mechanic replenish us for our race. This is what Habakkuk experienced in the final verse: the Lord restores his strength and allows him to keep on going like a fleet and frisky deer. Praising God is a key way to renew our strength and energy for the challenges of life.

How Should We Praise God?

We praise God by sharing everything openly and honestly with Him. Praise is not just telling God how wonderful and beautiful and powerful He is. It's not just expressing our thanks and appreciation for all He's done for us and given to us. We also praise Him by placing our needs daily in His hands through prayer—because when we pray and trust Him, we are acknowledging His love and His care for us. We praise God by sharing the junk with Him—the feelings of fear, discouragement, depression and worry that come to us. (It's not honoring to God when we try to be phony and pretend everything's great. How can He touch us inside if we're not willing to open ourselves up to Him?) We praise God even when we confess our sins to Him—because when we do so, we are renewing our faith in His mercy and forgiveness, so freely offered to all who will repent and receive it.

Finally, we praise God by living for Him and obeying Him in all aspects of our daily tasks. Though we face constant temptations to follow the impulses of our human nature and the enticements of the secular society around us, our Heavenly Father is pleased and honored and worshipped when we choose to do His will. A holy, devoted and faithful life—whatever our circumstances—is a powerful act of praise to God and of testimony to those around us.

Look Up

As I've been thinking about what it means to praise God when life stinks, I remembered a book I read several years ago. It was written by a young woman named Lisa Beamer. Her story, entitled *Let's Roll*, tells of her life with her husband Todd, one of the leaders of the courageous passengers who took back the cockpit of United Flight 93 on September 11 and put it down in a field in Pennsylvania, rather than allowing it to be a torpedo into the U.S. Capitol or the White House as the terrorists had intended.

How could a pregnant young woman—suddenly widowed and left to care for two small boys and a daughter on the way—possibly cope with the grief, the staggering responsibilities, the anger and questioning … and manage to do so in front of a watching nation? Yet she has—with grace, humility, and an unshakeable faith. This is how Lisa concludes her book:

> The pain is real, but so is the hope. Sometimes it's hard to live with both realities. For several weeks following September 11, I'd walk into Todd's closet, see his clothes, and start crying … The tears will show up often in my life, sometimes when I least expect them. I know that even years from now, when the acute pain subsides, there will still be twinges of sadness because Todd's not here to enjoy

life with us. But that's what life on this earth is—happiness mixed with sadness. True joy will never come here, but knowing it awaits me in eternity helps me progress through whatever life brings in the darkest of times. God has whispered two words to me over and over: *Look up* ... *Look up.* Through that quiet voice I'm reminded to look beyond my own little life to the Creator of the universe. Without fail, looking up brings peace to my soul.[2]

"Look up"—that's what it means to praise God. We can join Lisa Beamer in looking up even when life stinks. And what a difference that makes in our hearts and minds, and in our ability to cope!

Blooming Where We're Planted

JANUARY 31, 2010

*A tradition at First Church is the annual Kirkin' o' the Tartan,
a Sunday when, amid the skirl of bagpipes, we celebrate the Scottish roots
of the Presbyterian church. This was the Kirkin' message in 2010.*

By the rivers of Babylon we sat and wept
when we remembered Zion.
²There on the poplars
we hung our harps,
³for there our captors asked us for songs,
our tormentors demanded songs of joy;
they said, "Sing us one of the songs of Zion!"
⁴How can we sing the songs of the LORD
while in a foreign land?
⁵If I forget you, O Jerusalem,
may my right hand forget its skill.
⁶May my tongue cling to the roof of my mouth
if I do not remember you,
if I do not consider Jerusalem
my highest joy.
– PSALM 137:1-6

Janet's physician husband had been, for over a decade, a general surgeon and the head of the residency program at a suburban Boston teaching hospital. He was unexpectedly contacted by the University of Arizona School of Medicine in Tucson, and through a series of interviews was hired to be a professor and the head of the department of surgery. It was his dream job, an unanticipated answer to his prayers. He immediately left New England to get started in the new position, leaving Janet to pack up and market their house and arrange for the move. Once the moving van pulled out of their driveway headed southwest, she prepared her car for the long solitary drive across the North American continent. She loaded it up with a couple suitcases, books and music on CD's, and a beautiful plant her best friend Debbie had given her at her goodbye party. The long journey along the interstate highway gave Janet plenty of opportunity to cry through and pray through her emotions.

When she got to the new home in Tucson, everything was profoundly different. She didn't know anyone. Her husband was working incredibly long hours. The city and its culture and the stark desert scenery around her felt totally foreign—so unlike the rolling hills and the nearby Atlantic shoreline she had loved in New England. She tried to busy herself with setting up and moving into the house. The plant from Debbie that she had carried on the front seat as her companion on the long drive was given a place on their back patio, shaded from the hot desert sun, where Janet could water it and care for it and remember her friends by it.

One morning as she sat on her patio, praying and reading her Bible, missing her former home and relationships, and feeling a bit sorry for herself, she looked over at her plant. She noticed a new bloom popping out of it, and the leaves were shiny and green. Obviously this little potted plant had adapted quite well to its relocation. And that's when it hit Janet: God had given her that plant to teach her a lesson. Just as it was blooming in its new environment, so should she. That was an inner turning point. "Alright, Lord," she prayed. "You brought me here. I don't know why yet. But I'm willing to let you help me bloom in this new place."

Coping with Change

Changes come at intervals throughout our lives. And a long-distance move or relocation can be one of the hardest and most disruptive to us. The statistics on the mobility of the American people are staggering. The numbers for 2008 indicate that nearly 45 million people in our nation alone moved their place of residence that year—for at least part of the year, if not permanently.

Many of us have moved recently to this community from somewhere else. And many of us move at least twice a year, from a northern to a southern home and then back again. Some moves are much-desired and joyfully chosen. Other moves feel forced upon us, for a wide range of reasons. Sometimes we are excited about a move; other times we dread it and struggle to adjust to it, as our friend Janet did in her move to Tucson. Think about the incredible adjustments and inner turmoil that hundreds of thousands of Haitians have been experiencing in the past few weeks, as they have left the rubble of Port-au-Prince to head to the countryside or emigrate to another country.

Even the relocations we choose and initiate bring challenges with them. When we undertake them, we make choices that will lead us towards either growth or decline. A significant move can either prove to be a loss or an opportunity for positive enhancement.

We're thinking about the experience of moving and starting over for several reasons today. For one, Southwest Florida is a community made up primarily of people who have come from somewhere else. Secondly, in this annual Kirkin' o' the Tartan service, we are celebrating a nation and culture, originating in Scotland, that has spread worldwide and has had a phenomenal impact on continents and nations and peoples thousands of miles from the Scottish homeland. A third reason is that the history of God's Word and the spread of the Christian message is all about people who were on the move. And finally, we're talking about the experience of moving because, in many ways, the life of faith is one that takes us from one place to another—as Billy Graham describes in his final book, *The Journey*.

Our biblical text for today is Psalm 137. I find myself drawn again and again to the Psalms, the book that resides at the center of the Bible, because it speaks so honestly and powerfully to all the experiences and emotions of life. And sometimes the feelings expressed in the Psalms are pretty raw and unfiltered. That's what we find here.

The Babylonian Exile

The context that produced Psalm 137 was a devastating experience for many of the people of Israel: a forced move or relocation, away from their homes and the beautiful rolling hills of the Holy Land to the hot and hostile foreign country of Babylon (today's Iraq). This was definitely not a move this author had chosen. He had not purchased a retirement condo on the banks of the Euphrates River. Instead, he and many of his countrymen (the Jews) were being forcibly relocated. "Pack your suitcases," the conquering army of Nebuchadnezzar said. "We're taking you back with us to Babylon." And so the best and the brightest of a whole generation found themselves in a place they didn't choose. And at the time these words are written, they're obviously not adjusting very well to it.

"By the rivers of Babylon we sat and wept" (137:1). They looked back towards Mount Zion, the hill on which their beloved hometown of Jerusalem was set, and their hearts were broken. They wallowed in depression. Singing the old songs with the joy they once felt seemed impossible. They were determined to never adjust to this new place, to keep their minds locked onto a place—Jerusalem—that they would never see again in their lifetimes. Their plaintive grief is best summed up in verse 4: "How can we sing the songs of the LORD while in a foreign land?" And their emotions were answering: *We can't! It's impossible. There is no way we can bloom in this new place.*

God's Purposes

But these words are not the final chapter of their story. This is just their initial reaction. Though they thought all was lost, and concluded that God had abandoned and rejected them, and even had jumped to the assumption that the purpose of redemption would never be fulfilled, they were wrong. As we look back now, from the perspective of history, we can see that this unwanted move to Babylon is part of God's plan. And we can see His purposes in it.

Why did God allow His people to be taken far away for a generation, before returning them to resettle and rebuild their homeland? How could any good come of that? There were several reasons for this dramatic move.

God used the Jews to be a great blessing to the pagan empire of Babylon, the superpower of its day. Read the books of Daniel and Esther in the Old Testament and you will see how godly people, following the principles of Scripture, actually became powerful and influential among the great empires of the ancient world. Like a little salt that flavors meat or a little leaven that causes a loaf to rise, they had an impact.

God used the exile of the Jews to purify them and renew them spiritually; to give them a fresh start. As individuals, we can all get into some bad habits and ruts: in our jobs, our marriages, our personal habits and our physical lifestyle. The nation of Israel had drifted into a really bad rut. They needed to be lifted out of it dramatically. It was the fresh start that this unplanned relocation triggered that led to a great reawakening—and we read that story in the books of Nehemiah and Ezra and Haggai.

God used the process of scattering the Jewish people as a future strategy for what He intended to accomplish centuries later, when His plan for the redemption of mankind was completed by the coming of His Son. The apostles were sent out on their mission to take the Good News to the whole earth, and as Peter and Paul and John and the rest traveled by divine guidance, they found scattered colonies and synagogues of Jews in nearly every city across the ancient world. That was where their proclamation began. In effect, these pockets of Jews waiting for the Messiah became the fertile Petri dishes in which Christian churches were germinated. All through the Book of Acts, the brilliance of God's plan to first scatter the Jews, and then send the Gospel message to them, is reconfirmed.

God used the experience of His people in being relocated to help them discover that He is everywhere. The Lord of the Universe is not localized in any one place. The Jews discovered that they could talk to God in Babylon or Persia or Greece or Rome or Egypt, and He is the same God. He is, in fact, as much here in this place as anywhere. And wherever we go on earth, He is right there with us.

Imagining ourselves in the place of the writer of Psalm 137, we realize that he couldn't see all that God was going to do. This is what can happen to any of us: our immediate situation completely obscures our perspective. When we're down in a pit, we can't see out of it. And that's where faith comes in. That's why we need to be reminded that, even though we may feel grief or loneliness, sadness or fear, the Lord is still with us—and He will never abandon us. The classic mistake of the author of our psalm is so common. When a person moves—like our friend Janet, who had to pull up her New England roots and replant them in Arizona—the common mistake is to hold on to the past and to memories, to sink into feelings of grief and loss, and let those control us. What God wants us to do, instead, is to trust Him enough that we embrace and adapt to the present—knowing that His grace is sufficient for these new challenges.

A Nation on the Move

We celebrate the heritage and example of the nation of the Scots on this Sunday each year not primarily because we like bagpipe music, nor because we enjoy the colors of the tartans, nor because it's fun to see men wearing skirts. Those are really incidental. The real point we want to remember and celebrate and teach to subsequent generations is the way in which God's faithfulness is shown through those who trust in Him. That's why the Scottish heritage has had such a profound effect on the world. There were several waves of large-scale outward migrations from Scotland and the Scottish settlements of the northern half of Ireland. Some of the Scots chose to leave their beloved homeland to start a new life for themselves and their families. Others felt great pressures to leave, as in the periods known as the "Highland Clearances" in the 17th and 18th centuries, when English armies drove out many of the clans. Scots in large numbers moved across the waves to the New World of America and Canada, to southern Africa, and to Australia and New Zealand. The impact they had is well-documented in an outstanding book by historian Arthur Herman entitled *How the Scots Invented the Modern World*—and those of you who enjoy history might find it as fascinating and eye-opening as I did.

Why were the Scots so singularly effective in moving from one place to another and making such a difference? It is clear that they "bloomed where they were planted." They took their values, their courage, their determination and work ethic, and their faith, wherever they went. Though they took with them and cherished their love of their homeland, and their bagpipes and music, and their clans and tartans, they chose to not pine for their homeland in hopeless resignation and despair. They believed that their future could be as good as, or better than, their past—with God's help.

And I personally believe that this is the key to why the Scots could "bloom" so beautifully: because they were, as much as any nation the world has seen, a People of the Book. They were steeped in the Scriptures. All

Scottish children were taught to read, so that they could know this Book. The worship services of the Presbyterian and Reformed faith were built around the reading and proclamation of the Word of God. And they were a people of the whole book, not just the Old Testament. They understood how Jesus transformed and completed the plan of God, and the role He intended for them to carry out. Though in portions of the Old Testament it appears as if God is "circling the wagons" and pulling everything in towards Jerusalem, once the Cross and the Resurrection had been accomplished the direction moved dramatically and irreversibly outward.

Listen to these, the final words of Jesus in Matthew 28: "All authority in heaven and on earth has been given to me. Therefore go and make disciples of all nations, baptizing them ... and teaching them ... And surely I am with you always, to the very end of the age." They're not told to come back home to Jerusalem and stay there. Nor are they to weep and pine and complain, as the writer of Psalm 137, "How can we sing the LORD's song in a foreign land?" No, Jesus has put His song within us and has sent us out to sing it clearly and forcefully everywhere. And the Scots, informed by their New Testaments, went forward without fear. Because they had the final promise of their Lord to cling to and claim: "I am with you always." Wherever they went, the same God met them there and strengthened and sustained them.

Principles to Remember

As I close, I want us to think about what these truths mean to us. While some of us have been living where we are for a while and feel settled and comfortable, others of us know very well right now what it feels like to go through the disruptions and dislocations of a move. And some of us are moving frequently: ripping up the roots in one place and trying to replant them in another. Even when we choose to relocate, and look forward to it, there are still adjustments. There are the practical ones: how do I find a doctor, a car repairman, a dry cleaner, or a pizza parlor to replace what I left behind? And there are emotional adjustments as well: feeling lonely, feeling cut off from people and places we miss, feeling disoriented.

When those times of change come, remember these two principles from Scripture. First: the Lord has guaranteed—has pledged His name and His honor on the assurance—that He will always be with us. So we can turn to Him, read His Word, and pray to Him anytime and anywhere. And the second principle: people adapt to change better when they're connected to others in relationships than when they try to do it by themselves. If you're new to this community, you need a church. If this isn't the right one for you, don't quit looking till you find one and get involved in it. The Jews of the ancient world, when God scattered them, bonded together in fellowships called synagogues. The churches of the New Testament were built on the same model. You can be a Christian without being part of a church—but you can't be as effective and strong all by yourself as you can with others.

Conclusion

Some of us here are going through situations that are new and challenging to us—even if our street address hasn't changed for a long time. A change comes when a doctor diagnoses a disease or condition that limits or alters our lifestyle. Profound change can come when a family member dies, when a child moves away from home, when we lose a job, and when a time of volunteer service comes to an end. Change can, without a doubt, be very hard to adjust to—whether we're young or old or in-between.

But changes in life and our situation also bring opportunities to learn in a new way the basic lessons from God's Word. When all around us changes, we can choose to trust in God. When we find ourselves in a new place, we can choose to "bloom where we're planted."

The Meaning of 911

SEPTEMBER 11, 2011

In September First Church honors and thanks our community servants.
In this message, given on the 10th anniversary of 9/11/01,
Pastor Pratt reveals God's 911.

He who dwells in the shelter of the Most High
will rest in the shadow of the Almighty.
²I will say of the LORD, "He is my refuge and my fortress,
my God, in whom I trust."
³Surely he will save you from the fowler's snare
and from the deadly pestilence.
⁴He will cover you with his feathers,
and under his wings you will find refuge;
his faithfulness will be your shield and rampart.
⁵You will not fear the terror of night,
nor the arrow that flies by day,
⁶nor the pestilence that stalks in the darkness,
nor the plague that destroys at midday.
⁷A thousand may fall at your side,
ten thousand at your right hand,
but it will not come near you.

⁸You will only observe with your eyes
and see the punishment of the wicked.
⁹If you make the Most High your dwelling—
even the LORD, who is my refuge—
¹⁰then no harm will befall you,
no disaster will come near your tent.
¹¹For he will command his angels concerning you
to guard you in all your ways;
¹²they will lift you up in their hands,
so that you will not strike your foot against a stone.
¹³You will tread upon the lion and the cobra;
you will trample the great lion and the serpent.
¹⁴"Because he loves me," says the LORD, "I will rescue him;
I will protect him, for he acknowledges my name.
¹⁵He will call upon me, and I will answer him;
I will be with him in trouble, I will deliver him and honor him.
¹⁶With long life will I satisfy him
and show him my salvation."
– PSALM 91

In Case of Emergency

The numerical sequence 9-1-1 has had a special meaning for Americans for several decades now, since phone companies and state governments agreed to set up a standardized national call number for emergencies. This is the simple telephone number that children memorize and that adults of all ages depend on in an emergency. Whether we're in an auto accident, or our spouse feels crushing chest pains, or we smell smoke in our home or office, or we suspect an intruder has broken in, we quick dial those three digits.

We all have faced needs and emergencies (or will sometime in the future). How comforting it is to know that when we most require help, someone is on the other end of the line waiting to respond. This is, of course, why we have set aside a Sunday each year to honor and say "thanks" to our community servants, those who are trained and equipped to be at the other end of the 9-1-1 call.

A New Meaning

Ten years ago that same sequence of numbers took on an entirely different significance for us. And today we remember those terrible events of September 11, 2001—and how they impacted individuals, our country and our world. On that quiet morning unimaginable things happened, with broad impact:

- The sense of peace and stability our nation had felt through a decade since the end of the Cold War was shattered.
- People in the New York area and the Washington area, and elsewhere, suddenly lost loved ones—almost 3,000 men and women.
- Americans everywhere, in their homes and offices and schools, felt shock and panic and a compelling impulse to make sure those they loved were safe; thousands had their travel plans or work plans immediately altered.
- Many people took a hard look at their lives and priorities; some made temporary changes but lapsed back into their previous lifestyle, while others made permanent course corrections.
- We witnessed the hard work and sacrifice—and, in some cases, the ultimate sacrifice—of true heroes from fire departments and police forces who labored to respond to a disaster on an unimagined scale.

- In our anger and defiance, our nation experienced a rebirth of patriotism, as American flags sprouted everywhere.
- Our political leaders actually dropped their partisanship for a time and rallied together, singing *God Bless America* on the capitol steps without an aisle separating them, and gathering at the National Cathedral to humbly listen to the Word of God and pray together.

Many of us here today have personal and unforgettable memories of that day. How many of you were in New York City or Washington, D.C. when the airliners struck the Twin Towers and Pentagon? Were any of you traveling on that day and impacted by the cancellation of flights and the disruption of ordinary transportation? Did anyone here know personally someone who was killed or injured in New York or Washington, or in the plane that went down in the Pennsylvania farmland?

Magazines and newspapers, TV shows and blogs have been filled in the past week with personal reflections and reminiscences of that September morning and its aftermath. I just finished reading *Decision Points*, the memoirs of George W. Bush. None of us can ever imagine the kind of impact that day had on him, as he felt the personal burden of protecting 300 million Americans, as well as trying to defeat a shadowy enemy with no borders and no hesitation to employ the most inhumane tactics against the most innocent non-combatants. We can debate endlessly how well he did or did not do, but nobody would ever choose to be in that situation.

In reaching the 10-year anniversary, some of our journalists have lately been looking back on Americans' reactions to 9/11/01 as if it had been a great natural disaster to cope with, comparable in its emotional impact to Hurricane Katrina in 2005 along the northern Gulf of Mexico, or the earthquake and tsunami that devastated parts of Japan last March. But those are inaccurate comparisons, revealing historical near-sightedness. What September 11 actually felt like was not a natural disaster but an unprovoked act of war by a new enemy. Its closest emotional equivalent for our current generations may be the impact of Pearl Harbor sixty years earlier in 1941, an attack which catapulted our nation into a desperate struggle for survival.

In hindsight we can see (and give profound thanks) that no subsequent large-scale attacks have occurred on American civilians in ten years. But we couldn't imagine that at the time. We had every reason to think that terror would become a continual reality for us. And the war against radical Islamic extremists has still taken a heavy toll, in Iraq and Afghanistan, in Israel, and in some other democratic countries like England and Spain and India. The vigilance of security forces and the blunders of amateur terrorists (like the "underwear bomber" and the "Times Square bomber," who both failed), have combined, by God's grace, to prevent subsequent attacks. But even with enhanced security, there is no 100% guarantee of our future safety. Some of us are praying daily for young men and women who are serving in our military and are seeking to defend us and defeat extremism in dangerous places.

The Biblical 911

The digital sequence of 911 brings many powerful thoughts to us from the past decade. But for centuries and millennia before our time, this number has meant something very different for believers. Psalm 91:1 is "God's 911," the answer to our call for help: "He who dwells in the shelter of the Most High will rest in the shadow of the Almighty." It is the Lord's invitation to each of us to live a life of trust and faith, surrender and obedience. Let's look first at what Psalm 91 says.

Verses 1 and 2 talk about a choice and its consequences. The choice is one to place absolute and eternal trust, confidence and faith in the great God, the Almighty Creator and Lord, the Hebrew name *El Shaddai* (God Most High). This decision is described as "dwelling" in God. It means a decision to move into Him, to commit to Him as the permanent residence of your soul. This had special meaning for the Hebrews, a people who were descended from nomads. Nomads live in tents, constantly on the move, never knowing a place that they can truly call "home." A place of permanence is what every nomad longs for. I personally suspect that this psalm may have been written by or for people who were living a nomadic life, or who were on a long journey. Why? Because verse 10 talks about people who live in tents. And while we may not literally live in tents, our "residence" here on earth is no less temporary … for in this life we are simply travelers and pilgrims passing through on our way to a final destiny. The home we all seek is called heaven, and we can experience a foretaste of that permanent security, peace and rest even in the midst of our life's travels if we place our faith in the Lord.

Verses 3 through 8 are a creative way of picturing the security that God brings to His people. The author alternates two images or comparisons: he imagines himself as a soldier at war, and as a baby bird. Look at how God is described as caring for both.

- Verse 3—The bird will be saved from the "fowler's snare." A fowler is one who tries to trap birds. Similarly, the soldier will be protected from the "deadly pestilence." In the ancient world, far more troops died of disease in camp than died in battle; the close quarters and the lousy sanitation could allow bubonic plague or typhoid fever to decimate an army.
- Verse 4—The baby bird is covered by its mother's feathers, and nestles for rest and warmth under her wings. The soldier will find safety in combat from his own shield, and from hiding behind a wall or rampart for defense.
- Verse 5—The bird is protected by its mother from owls and other nighttime predators. The soldier is protected by his shield from the arrows launched by his enemy in battle.

- Verses 6 and 7—These verses refer to more protection for the soldier, from the plague and diseases of camp, and the deadly
weapons of combat.

After these alternating pictures of God's protection for those who find
themselves in a dangerous place (like a baby bird emerging into a world of
predators, or a soldier marching off to the uncertainties of warfare), we
have in verses 9 through 13 a description of what happens beyond the scope
of our eyesight in the unseen spiritual world. There's a lot more going on
in the universe than our senses can perceive or our scientific instruments
measure. And in this passage we have a description of both the spiritual
powers of good (the angels, who are servants and representatives of God,
sent to aid and protect His own) and the powers of evil (the devil and his
wicked demons, constantly on the prowl to attack us through every means
available).

Angels, the Bible tells us, are real, though our eyes can't see them.
And we will never know how many times, and in how many ways, they
have helped and protected and rescued us in our lifetimes, until our moment comes to leave this earth. The Bible also says that personalized evil is
real. We know that Satan is being described here, because the Evil One
Himself actually quoted verses 11-12 to Jesus while he was tempting our
Savior to do something reckless and foolish. But the devil pointedly did
not quote verse 13—and for good reason: it speaks of his own ultimate defeat and destruction. The two creatures Satan is compared to in scripture
are the serpent and the lion. The wonderful assurance of verse 13 is that
those who trust in God will, in the end, triumph over evil: "You will tread
upon the lion and the cobra [that is, the devil]; you will trample the great
lion and the serpent."

The psalm ends with assurance that God's protection will be with us.
What we find only dim hints about, though, is the fullness of God's promise
of eternal life. We are told in the final verse that He will "show us salvation."

It is in the New Testament, in the words of Jesus and His apostles, that we have this great hope spelled out for us in much greater detail and certainty.

The Experiences of Life

Let's think about what the words of this psalm mean to us. An American Christian in the year 2011 cannot pretend that life is all sweetness and joy and comfort and goodness. It's a dangerous, uncertain and at times evil world we live in. How do we make sense of what happened last week … last month … last year … or ten years ago?

How do we see the hand of a loving God and His ultimate purposes for good in the midst of a world of suicide bombers, child kidnappers, freakish natural disasters (floods and forest fires, storms and earthquakes)? How do we discern the redemption that is promised to God's people when Christians die every day of disease or violence or accident?

The experiences of life come to us uninterpreted. Things happen, and we have to figure out what they mean. Lots of people interpret and draw conclusions from their own personal experiences that lead them into great misery and unhappiness. A woman who was abused by her father concludes she will never trust a man again. A person who was ill-treated by an employer concludes life is unfair. A person who prayed for healing and did not receive it concludes there is no God. The radicals of Al-Qaeda drew the wrong conclusion about America, and about the purpose of life. If you don't get the right interpretation, you'll make the wrong choices of how to respond to events.

In the year 1799 a French archaeologist digging in Egypt near the town of Rosetta made an amazing discovery in the sand. He found a tablet, since named "The Rosetta Stone," that had inscriptions in three languages, including ancient Egyptian hieroglyphics. For over a thousand years, people had puzzled over the meaning of that strange picture alphabet, carved in the pyramids, tombs and temples of the Pharaohs. People made guesses about the language, but had no way of knowing. The Rosetta Stone changed that, because it allowed scholars to compare a known language—ancient Greek—with its translation into the Egyptian writing. Finally the code to understanding hieroglyphics was cracked.

Interpreted through Scripture

I believe the Bible is the great Rosetta Stone for human experience. It helps us understand and interpret what otherwise is indecipherable to us. It shows us reality, as God sees it, and truths we can rely upon. Here are a few essential truths Psalm 91 helps us to see and which, in turn, help us to interpret and make sense of the seemingly confusing and random events of our world.

The Bible tells us that nothing which is visible to our eyes can ever give us lasting security. Stock in a growth company won't make us secure, because stock markets can crash. Physical strength and athletic skill won't make us secure, because the advance of age is ultimately undefeated. Our intellect is not enough to give us eternal confidence, for memories can be destroyed by Alzheimer's. Nothing inside this world can give us unending security. That can only come to us from outside the world, from the One who invites us to "dwell" in Him and "rest" within His "shadow."

The Bible assures us that nothing can happen to shake a Christian's spiritual security. No danger or harm will come to us outside of God's will, once we place ourselves in the Lord's almighty hands. We do, of course, live in a dangerous place. But when it's not our time, God through His spiritual powers beyond our measuring will protect us, bring us through "many dangers, toils and snares" (as the hymn says) and give us the strength to cope with the pains of body, mind and emotions we encounter. And when our time does come at last (in some cases, sooner rather than later), the Lord offers to everyone the incomparable promise of eternal life. On a Tuesday morning in September ten years ago, nearly 3,000 people woke up to what they assumed would be another typical day. They raced unthinking to airports and office buildings, little knowing that within hours their earthly lives would be over and their future destinies would begin—for good or ill.

The Bible tells us that nothing we do in keeping with God's purposes is in vain. Not long ago there was a gathering of some of the widows of men who died in the World Trade Center, along with some of their children who had lost their fathers. It was apparently quite a touching time, and also a reminder that there is much to live for even after tragedy. One young Christian woman had waited in vain for her husband (a manager at Cantor Fitzgerald, whose office was near the top of the North Tower) to come home on that fateful day. She reflected on how her loss had changed her outlook on life:

> I used to rush my life. I was always saying, "I can't wait for Christmas, I can't wait for vacation." Now I wish I had spent more time enjoying every moment, as my husband always told me to do. Now I won't see him again until I get to heaven. But I am trying to live each day I have left to the fullest, to make him proud of me on that day when we are reunited.

May we also live like that, resting continuously in our faith in the Almighty's security and protection!

Finding an Older Brother

FEBRUARY 26, 2012

*Pastor Pratt's messages often reference current events, local
and national developments and significant happenings at First Church.
This sermon, in its mention of Louie Zamperini, remembers
our most popular Bonita Christian Forum speaker to date,
and also, interestingly, sets the stage for our focus on
The Parable of the Prodigal Son (in art and music) in March 2014.*

*Now the tax collectors and sinners were all gathering around to hear
Jesus. ²But the Pharisees and the teachers of the law muttered, "This man
welcomes sinners and eats with them." …*

*¹¹Jesus continued: "There was a man who had two sons. ¹²The younger
one said to his father, 'Father, give me my share of the estate.' So he divided
his property between them.*

*¹³"Not long after that, the younger son got together all he had, set off
for a distant country and there squandered his wealth in wild living…*

²⁰"So he got up and went to his father.

*"But while he was still a long way off, his father saw him and was filled
with compassion for him; he ran to his son, threw his arms around him and
kissed him.*

21"The son said to him, 'Father, I have sinned against heaven and against you. I am no longer worthy to be called your son.'

22"But the father said to his servants, 'Quick! Bring the best robe and put it on him. Put a ring on his finger and sandals on his feet. 23Bring the fattened calf and kill it. Let's have a feast and celebrate. 24For this son of mine was dead and is alive again; he was lost and is found.' So they began to celebrate.

25"Meanwhile, the older son was in the field. When he came near the house, he heard music and dancing. 26So he called one of the servants and asked him what was going on. 27'Your brother has come,' he replied, 'and your father has killed the fattened calf because he has him back safe and sound.'

28"The older brother became angry and refused to go in. So his father went out and pleaded with him. 29But he answered his father, 'Look! All these years I've been slaving for you and never disobeyed your orders. Yet you never gave me even a young goat so I could celebrate with my friends. 30But when this son of yours who has squandered your property with prostitutes comes home, you kill the fattened calf for him!'" – FROM LUKE 15

Brothers and Opposites

How could two siblings be so different? How could they start out at an identical place in life and end up in such radically different destinations? Two people (two brothers or two sisters, for example) who have the exact same mother and father, the exact same home and hometown, the same DNA, the same basic schooling, the same rules and discipline, can nevertheless be as different as night and day, as opposite as arctic tundra and tropical rain forest. How does it happen? It's one of the great mysteries in life.

Two brothers came from a tiny town in the south, the sons of a peanut farmer. One of them was named Jimmy, and the other Billy. Jimmy, the older brother, was the classic over-achiever: a star student and star athlete in school, he won an appointment to the U.S. Naval Academy and then was commissioned and served as a Naval officer in the fledging U.S. Nuclear Submarine program. Billy, the younger brother, struggled in school; he enrolled at Emory University under pressure from his family, but quickly dropped out and never finished his education.

After the Navy Jimmy became a successful farmer and businessman, and then felt the nudge in his late 40's to enter politics. He was elected as a State Senator in Georgia, and then as the Governor of the state. Stunningly, he defied all the political odds to be elected as the 39th President of the United States. In his retirement, Jimmy Carter has been active in numerous causes (some of them rather controversial). He is one of only four surviving ex-Presidents. He has been a vocal Christian, and no one has ever questioned his personal morality or integrity.

Billy Carter, on the other hand, had a checkered career of frequent failures. He was best known for owning a gas station; his only attempt at politics was running for Mayor of Plains, Georgia—an election he lost resoundingly. Billy was a beer-guzzler, frequently in trouble with the law, the classic stereotype of the lazy "good ol' boy," and in 1988 he died of cancer at the young age of 51. How could two brothers be more different?

What about your family? Are you different in personality or in life's choices from one of your siblings? Do any two of your children or grandchildren show striking differences? It's part of the mystery of free will and human choice. The same genes don't make us the same people.

There are intriguing examples in the Bible of this same paradox. Jacob and Esau, the twin sons of Isaac, were like a cat and a dog: totally opposite. The Apostle Peter's brother Andrew was nothing like him. And here, in our text for today—one of the best-known and best-loved of the stories Jesus told—we have another reminder of how two brothers could turn out quite differently.

The Parable and its Context

This tale is often given the name "The Parable of the Prodigal Son." But that is a flawed title, because it's really the story of two sons. These two brothers are as opposite as Jimmy and Billy Carter. And most significantly, they are both alienated from their father (though in different ways). The spiritual meaning of the story is that both of the sons are equally lost, and equally in need of redemption and reconciliation to God. Those of you who have read the wonderful little book *The Prodigal God* by Tim Keller,[3] which was our summer book two years ago, will recognize and be reminded of these insights—and I want to acknowledge my gratitude to Tim for helping to make this story come alive so beautifully.

Let's remember the context of Luke 15. People who had some major problems and issues in their lives were responding eagerly to the proclamation of the Word of God. For years these men and women had felt like they were not welcome in church. And although they had each made a lot of bad choices in their lives, they at least recognized that they had needs and flaws. They were somehow drawn to this Jesus of Nazareth the way bugs are drawn to a porch light on a hot summer night.

The Pharisees, on the other hand, were as self-righteous, arrogant and contented a group as we've ever seen. They were watching from a distance with superiority and judgment, their arms crossed over their chests in disgust, their noses held high in the air with disdain. "Church is for religious people," they believed. "You have to clean up your act first if you ever want God to approve of you. How lucky God is to have such exemplary people as us to be role models! And if this Jesus of Nazareth actually cares about that filth, those low-life losers, then he is clearly not up to our caliber."

Rule-Breakers and Rule-Keepers

The scene is now set for Jesus to tell a simple but timeless story. How many millions of times through the centuries has it been repeated in one family after another? One child—in this case the younger, though not always—is the free-spirited, undisciplined, pleasure-seeking rebel. He set himself on a course of self-discovery, and blunders into one disastrous consequence after another. We'll label him the "Rule-Breaker." The other brother, the older one in this family, is the achiever, the obedient child, the one who tries to work the system rather than rebelling against it. We'll label him the "Rule-Keeper."

Which one can you best relate to? Which of the two highways of life have you most often traveled down? Here's my assessment: Most churches are filled with "Older Brothers"! And I'll bet we have more of that kind than the other here today.

A superficial look at this story might lead us to believe that the Older Brother is the hero and the Younger Brother the villain in the story. But it's much more complicated than that. Certainly the Younger Brother messes up his life and, in the process, does some unspeakable things to hurt his Father. When he demands his inheritance early, he is really saying, "Dad, I wish you were dead." And by taking his fortune and leaving his home, he is rejecting his entire family. The Father would have every right to kick the son out of the home without a cent, and to refuse to ever speak to him again. Of course the Father did not do that. Rather, when the Younger Son realized the mess he'd made of his life and turned back towards home, he was greeted there by his Father with extraordinary love and forgiveness and grace and restoration.

Mistakes of the Older Brother

But the story doesn't end with the forgiveness of the Younger. It has an entire Chapter Two that we must not miss—especially those of us who are more temperamentally wired to be "Rule-Keepers" than "Rule-Breakers." We discover that the Older Son, though always obedient and respectful, has mistakenly been trying to earn his Father's approval by his hard work and efforts. The tender heart of the Father, a heart of unconditional love and grace, has never penetrated or been reflected in the hard, self-centered and unforgiving heart of the Older Son. All who follow in this path become, whether we want to admit it or not, Pharisees. Whenever we get to thinking that God "owes" us because we've been "good," or that we are better than others because we're smarter or more religious or better behaved than they are, we have fallen into a ditch of our own digging.

That is Mistake #1 by the Older Brother. Be on guard against that oh-so-common attitude that we earn God's blessing and care. It is either a gift or it's nothing. But there is a Mistake #2 we also need to recognize. Tim Keller brilliantly explains this in *The Prodigal God*, and it would have been something that everyone who first heard this story would have immediately and instinctively recognized. In the Middle Eastern culture of its time, the Older Brother in any family had special privileges but also special responsibilities. The privileges included being heir to the largest part of the family estate and becoming the patriarch someday. The burden of responsibility was a weighty one. The first-born son needed to be "his brothers' and sisters' keeper." Their welfare was supposed to be his highest concern.

When the ancient family operated as it was intended to, the Older Brother would operate in perfect harmony and consistency with the will of the Father. If one of his siblings was in need, he would be expected to sacrifice to help them. In the context of the story in Luke 15, therefore, we find that the Older Brother has not at all been the "perfect son" that he has imagined himself to be. He has actually been selfish and self-absorbed. If he had been a true Older Brother, he would have traveled around the earth if needed, paid any price, and made any sacrifice to find his Younger Brother, and rescue him. In effect, the Older Brother, when necessary, was to serve as the Redeemer of the family.

This Older Brother, however, completely fails in his most sacred responsibility. He doesn't seek out and redeem his lost Younger Brother. Instead, he wipes his hands of him. "Good riddance. Who needs that brat?" And he stayed, comfortable and secure, in their home—while his Father's heart broke with the loss.

That was the attitude of the Pharisees towards their fellow Jews who had failed to keep the voluminous laws, rules and regulations the hyper-religious had demanded of them. The Older Brothers among the Pharisees looked at those who were struggling with the same superiority and selfish disdain as the Older Brother in the story. "Let them eat pig slop. Let them ruin their lives. Then they can be doubly punished by a stern and judgmental God, and that will show them!"

A True Older Brother

But now we come to the greatest part of the story. It's not found in the text of Luke 15; it is about to play itself out in the rest of the Gospel of Luke, and in all the other books of the New Testament. Here's the most dramatic plot twist of all. You and I have a True Older Brother. His name is Jesus. He came to fulfill the role that the Older Brother in the story failed to do. He has come to seek us, to redeem us, and to bring us back home to our Father. The costly work was done on the cross. Our Older Brother stretched out His arms and let them drive nails through them, for you and for me.

And so we find that we are all truly equal. The ones among us who have tried to find pleasure and fulfillment through breaking all the rules, and the ones among us who have tried to find praise and approval by following all the rules, are equally needy. We all need a Redeemer. And we have One, the great Older Brother for the human race.

Restoration to the Father

Picture in your mind those two brothers: one killing himself by his foolish choices and actions, the other consumed by hate and lack of forgiveness for his sibling. Both are alienated from their unconditionally loving and compassionate Father.

And now return with me to the year 1949 in Los Angeles, California. A huge tent set up on an empty lot is filled with thousands of people. The most reluctant man in that tent one night is named Louie Zamperini. In a final attempt to try to save a marriage that is on the brink of divorce, he agreed to go with his pleading wife. Louie is a man filled with raging demons. He has been drinking himself into a stupor almost daily for over a year. Every night he is haunted by nightmares of the sadistic Japanese prison guard who brutalized him day after day in his years of captivity. He is consumed with hatred and fantasies of revenge. Everything and everyone around him prompts him to rage, which prompts him to drink, in a hopeless downward spiral.

You could actually say that Louie was, at that moment, acting as both the Younger Brother and the Older Brother in the parable of Luke 15. He was self-destructing by his disastrous drinking, and he was consumed with bitterness and an unforgiving heart. It was a toxic mix and a dangerous moment, until Billy Graham stood up to speak.

Graham spoke clearly and unmistakably about the spiritual need we all have, and that we have all sinned. Author Laura Hillenbrand recounts this pivotal moment:

> Louie felt indignant rage flaring in him, a struck match. *I am a good man*, he thought. *I am a good man.* Even as he had this thought, he felt the lie in it. He knew what he had become.[4]

A living seed was planted that night. The next night he returned. As Billy Graham spoke, Louie in his mind went back to the raft, adrift in the

Pacific. It was the moment he thought he was about to die of thirst. He prayed, "God, if you save me, I will serve you forever." And then the rain started to fall. Back in the tent, he heard the rain beginning to fall outside. It was the sign he needed. Graham asked people to come forward to receive God's abundant, undeserved grace. Louie stepped to the aisle and started forward.

> Cynthia kept her eyes on Louie all the way home. When they entered the apartment, Louie went straight to the cache of liquor. It was the time of night when the need took hold of him, but for the first time in years, Louie had no desire to drink. He carried the bottles to the kitchen sink, opened them, and poured their contents into the drain. Then he hurried through the apartment, gathering packs of cigarettes, a secret stash of girlie magazines, everything that was part of his ruined years. He heaved it all down the trash chute.
>
> In the morning he woke feeling cleansed. For the first time in five years, the Bird hadn't come into his dreams. The Bird would never come again.
>
> Louie felt profound peace. What resonated with him now was not all that he had suffered but the divine love that he believed had intervened to save him. He was not the worthless, broken, forsaken man that the Bird had striven to make of him. In a single, silent moment, his rage, his fear, his humiliation and helplessness had fallen away. That morning, he believed, he was a new creation.[5]

No matter how good or bad we think we are, no matter what we've done or haven't done, we all need a Savior. We need an Older Brother to redeem us and show us the path of real love. And once we've found that Older Brother, we want to model our lives after Him, by forgiving others and helping them to find their way home.

If Christ
Never Came

DECEMBER 15, 2013

*Have you ever taken a closer look at something familiar
only to discover a treasure previously hidden?
In this sermon Pastor Pratt highlights a few key words…
that make all the difference.*

*"If the world hates you, keep in mind that it hated me first. ¹⁹If you be-
longed to the world, it would love you as its own. As it is, you do not belong
to the world, but I have chosen you out of the world. That is why the world
hates you. ²⁰Remember what I told you: 'A servant is not greater than his
master.' If they persecuted me, they will persecute you also. If they obeyed my
teaching, they will obey yours also. ²¹They will treat you this way because of
my name, for they do not know the one who sent me. ²²If I had not come and
spoken to them, they would not be guilty of sin; but now they have no excuse
for their sin." – JOHN 15:18-22*

Alternative Histories

Less than two months ago, veteran political journalist Jeff Greenfield published his newest book: *If Kennedy Lived*. Released to coincide with the 50th anniversary of the JFK assassination in Dallas, it is the latest in a tradition of what is known as "alternative history." Greenfield poses some fascinating questions. How might the events of our lifetimes turn out differently, and how would the world we live in be different today, if that shocking act of violence in 1963 had not triggered dramatic convulsions in American political life? If the bullets had missed him, what would the remainder of Kennedy's first term been like? Would he have been re-elected, and if so, what would he have done in a second term? Would the Vietnam War or the Cold War have followed different courses? Would Lyndon Johnson have been cut from the ticket? Would Kennedy's marital indiscretions ultimately have led to public scandal (as with President Clinton)?

Many writers have tried to exercise their imaginations along similar veins. I have read alternative histories of the Civil War, imagining that Lee had been victorious at Gettysburg, his troops had wheeled south towards Washington, and Lincoln's government had sued for peace. We would now have to show passports at the Mason-Dixon Line, Florida would be part of the Confederate States of America, and blacks would be second-class citizens or worse.

I have read alternative histories of the Second World War, imagining that Hitler had defeated Stalin and annexed the western half of Russia, and the mighty German war machine had turned western Europe into an impregnable fortress—preventing D-Day and the liberation of France and the Low Countries. We would have never had a Cold War against Communism, but we may have had a Cold War, or an extended Hot War, against Fascism.

It's all quite fascinating, and a bit chilling, to think about "what if..." Hollywood screenwriters have followed the same trail. In 2000 actor Nicolas Cage starred in a film called *The Family Man*, in which a single and work-obsessed Wall Street investment banker is given a glimpse of what his life could have been like, had he married his girlfriend 13 years earlier and chosen a more humble set of aspirations. And, of course, the classic "What if..." film is Frank Capra's *It's a Wonderful Life*, where George Bailey is shown by Clarence the guardian angel (who hadn't yet earned his wings) what his hometown of Bedford Falls would have been like if he had never been born.

I've always enjoyed these kinds of imaginative speculations. And I have found myself at times wondering about my own personal journey through life. How would I be different today, and how would others who are now part of my life be different, if I had chosen a different path? Perhaps you've wondered that as well. The ending of the famous Robert Frost poem sums up the amazing power of choices:

> *Two roads diverged in a wood, and I—*
> *I took the one less traveled by,*
> *and that has made all the difference.*

But a couple weeks ago, with the Advent and Christmas season looming on the horizon, I was reading through a portion of the Gospel of John for my morning reflections. I stumbled (as if on an unnoticed rock or tree root along a forest trail) over verse 22 of our text. Jesus, speaking to His closest friends the night before He went to the cross, said to them, "**If I had not come...**"

What If Christmas Had Never Happened?

Though I've probably read John chapter 15 a dozen times or more, I'd never really noticed that hypothetical statement. But this time it suddenly struck me: *What if* Christ had never come to earth? *What if* Christmas had never happened? *What if* the New Testament had never been written (for, of course, this entire book is all about One Man, Jesus of Nazareth —what He said and did and His impact on this world)? What if the land of Narnia, as described by C.S. Lewis in his fantasy novel *The Lion, the Witch and the Wardrobe*—in which all creation was under the power of the evil white witch and was "always winter but never Christmas"—was, in fact, a spiritual description of Planet Earth now? What would life be like today if there had been no Christmas?

Let's start with the obvious and immediate: the contemporary Christmas celebration. There would be no Christmas carols, because there was nothing to write songs about. There would be no manger scenes on church lawns, on Christmas cards, on postage stamps. There would be no Christmas trees (which were first introduced, according to legend, by Martin Luther to remind Christians of the eternal life—the evergreen—that Christ came to bring, with lights on the branches to testify to Him as the Light of the World). There would be no Santa Claus or "Saint Nicholas"—a great 3rd century Christian leader who expressed the love of Christ by secretly taking gifts to the homes of people in need and leaving them in the middle of the night.

And speaking of gifts, undoubtedly our retailers and manufacturers would have tried to come up with some other excuse for buying and gift-giving. Maybe, if there had been no Christmas, people today would give each other New Year's gifts and cards. Maybe somebody would have invented a New Year's character comparable to Saint Nicholas.

Maybe a completely secular society, with no churches and no Christian traditions, would have found some other reason to party and feast and interrupt the busy flow of the world for a short time. But if Christ never came, there would be no Christmas as we know it.

Let's dig deeper, though, beneath the surface of our contemporary

Christmas traditions. How would life be different 365 days a year if Christ had not come? There would be no Christian foundation for morality and laws in western society. The world into which He entered, like a bright starburst on a dark night, was one in which power and wealth ruled. The Roman Empire was a brutal place, a crude police state. The Roman oppressors (and their collaborators in the conquered provinces like Judea and Galilee) were ruthless. The values of love, of human rights, of cooperation and tolerance and understanding, of a law higher than the decree of the Emperor to which even the Emperor was subject: these concepts were completely unknown, even inconceivable. The "gods," whatever they were, had no relevance to daily life.

All that we cherish and hold dear in American society—liberty, community, love, mutual respect and due process of law—would not exist if there had been no Christian church. Western society, without the revolutionary overthrow of values from within that eventually changed the Roman Empire, would likely have been dominated by the violence and cruelty of paganism. Either the Romans would have continued to rule, or they would have been supplanted by even more ruthless and cutthroat Vikings or Huns or Mongols or Turks. Our constitution and laws are built on a biblical foundation … and that foundation would have never been laid if Christ had not come.

Let's dig even deeper, back further into time. The Old Testament would become a dead and lifeless book. It is, of course, the storybook of the Ancient Hebrews—who for thousands of years carried on this strange conviction that they were special people chosen by an all-powerful God, with a special purpose in the world. Though they strayed often from God's ways and were punished for their disobedience, yet one shining hope sustained them through the centuries. One day, prophet after prophet assured them, God would send a Messiah to them. He would be a direct descendant of the great King David, and would conquer death and live forever. He

Himself would fulfill all the requirements of the righteous divine law. Somehow He would also provide a way for the sins of all the people to be forgiven.

This promise—this guarantee—runs so strongly through the Old Testament that you cannot miss it. All of the prophecies are waiting to be fulfilled. Even the last chapter of the last book of the Old Testament, Malachi, ends with a hope that one day a great prophet like Elijah would return to proclaim that the Messiah had come. And then, silence—400 years or more of silence, to be precise—with no prophetic word. But if Jesus of Nazareth had not come to fulfill every Old Testament promise, and knit together in His own life and death and resurrection all the various strands of prophecies, then the Old Testament would be a book of dashed hopes and dreams. It would stand as a cruel monument to the delusions of a people. If the prophesies of the Messiah were lies, then who can believe *anything* in this Book?

Let's dig one layer even deeper. Like the oil and gas drillers who send their drill bits down into the ground through one vein of soil or rock after another until they strike the deep buried fuel, we're going to penetrate all the way down to the core of human nature. What would we humans be like today, if Christ had never come to earth? There would be no hope for humanity.

The Core Problem

To discover why we would have no reason for hope, we have to look at mankind's condition after sin and pride and selfishness entered into our hearts and souls. The story of the first humans in Genesis—whether you picture it as a precisely historical account or symbolic of all mankind—portrays the grim reality. We are separated from God and cannot experience fellowship with Him. We are all carrying a guilty conscience, with self-inflicted wounds from our own stubborn and disobedient choices—

and even if we haven't been schooled in formal ethics, we all know basic right from wrong. We are alienated from other humans, and our conflicting wants and desires repeatedly spoil human fellowship. That is the human condition.

And it is the core problem Jesus came to solve. The Old Testament imagery is of an innocent sacrifice that takes the place of the guilty to pay for a crime and restore fellowship between the alienated parties. Other images are used throughout the New Testament:

- Christ has paid the ransom by His own life, to free us from captivity to sin and death.
- Christ has adopted us into the family of God.
- Christ has healed us of our fatal, deadly disease.
- Christ has paid off the astronomical debt we have accumulated and could never hope to pay.

None of these have happened if Christmas never occurred. You and I would not be forgiven. We would not have the hope and confidence of eternal life. We would not have the peace of God within us to comfort us in every trial. God would remain distant, remote and unapproachable. The world would remain in the darkness of sin, and that darkness would penetrate into every heart.

Thus we can see the importance of an event that occurred in real time and place and history by logically identifying how subsequent events would be different if those events had not happened. What would be the consequences? And we see, set out clearly in the harsh spotlight of alternative history, that the event of Christmas had a profound and dramatic impact on humanity. Though many today may try to minimize, or trivialize, or sentimentalize the dramatic turning point at Bethlehem, its importance remains undeniable.

What Matters Most

We don't really know the exact date (or even the season of the year) when Christ was born. Church tradition for over a thousand years has become centered on late December, and finally a group of churches decided to arbitrarily set the date of the "Christ Mass" or celebration of His birth as December 25. There is some evidence, however, that indicates He may have actually been born in the springtime, not in December; but no one knows for sure. There are no birth certificates available. Our numbering of years may also be slightly off: the monks who re-dated our calendars during the Middle Ages probably slightly miscalculated, so that Jesus was likely born in about 5 or 4 or 3 B.C., not the year 1 A.D.

Late December was possibly adopted by the early churches in northern European countries in order to co-opt a pagan mid-winter festival. Each day through the months we now call November and December, the hours of daylight gradually decrease; it would appear to an observer that, in fact, the sun must be dying. But then, by the very end of the month (approximately December 25), it becomes obvious that the trend has reversed and the hours of daylight are increasing. And so the ancient pagans would celebrate the "rebirth of the sun." Christians, wanting to redirect their new converts from nature worship, may have seized upon this holiday and transformed it from the "rebirth of the sun" to the "Birth of the Son."

What matters to us is not exactly when this great miracle of Christ's coming to earth occurred, but *that* it occurred. And for Christians, what matters is not just the historic event, but its personal relevance and meaning. You and I celebrate not only that Christ was born in Bethlehem, but also that, in a spiritual sense, He is born into us. As His heavenly light pierced the literal darkness, so the light of understanding and faith has flooded into our dark minds to show us the truth. As He came to be the world's Savior, so He also offers to be a personal Savior—your Savior, and mine.